ARCHANGELS
& ASCENDED
MASTERS

Also by Doreen Virtue, Ph.D.

Books

Audio Programs

ANGELS AMONG US (with Michael Toms)
MESSAGES FROM YOUR ANGELS (abridged audio book)
PAST-LIFE REGRESSION WITH THE ANGELS
DIVINE PRESCRIPTIONS
THE ROMANCE ANGELS
CONNECTING WITH YOUR ANGELS (2-tape set and 6-tape set)
MANIFESTING WITH THE ANGELS
KARMA RELEASING
HEALING YOUR APPETITE, HEALING YOUR LIFE
HEALING WITH THE ANGELS
DIVINE GUIDANCE
CHAKRA CLEARING

Oracle Cards

(44 divination cards and guidebook)

HEALING WITH THE ANGELS ORACLE CARDS
HEALING WITH THE FAIRIES ORACLE CARDS
MESSAGES FROM YOUR ANGELS ORACLE CARDS
MAGICAL MERMAIDS AND DOLPHINS ORACLE CARDS
ARCHANGEL ORACLE CARDS

All of the above are available at your local
bookstore, or may be ordered by visiting:
Hay House USA: **www.hayhouse.com**
Hay House Australia: **www.hayhouse.com.au**
Hay House UK: **www.hayhouse.co.uk**
or Hay House South Africa: **orders@psdprom.co.za**

Doreen Virtue's Website:
AngelTherapy.com

ARCHANGELS & ASCENDED MASTERS

A Guide to Working and Healing with Divinities and Deities

Doreen Virtue, Ph.D.

HAY HOUSE, INC.

Carlsbad, California
London • Sydney • Johannesburg
Vancouver • Hong Kong • New Delhi

Copyright © 2003 by Doreen Virtue

Published and distributed in the United States by: Hay House, Inc.: www.hayhouse.com •
Published and distributed in Australia by: Hay House Australia Pty. Ltd.: www.hayhouse.com.au
• **Published and distributed in the United Kingdom by:** Hay House UK, Ltd.: www.hayhouse.co.uk
• **Published and distributed in the Republic of South Africa by:** Hay House SA (Pty), Ltd.:
orders@psdprom.co.za • Distributed in Canada by: Raincoast: www.raincoast.com • **Published
in India by:** Hay House Publications (India) Pvt. Ltd.: www.hayhouseindia.co.in • **Distributed
in India by:** Media Star: booksdivision@mediastar.co.in

Editorial supervision: Jill Kramer   *Design:* Jenny Richards

On the cover: Guinevere, the Celtic goddess of love relationships, fertility, and motherhood

Library of Congress Cataloging-in-Publication Data

Virtue, Doreen
 Archangels and ascended masters : a guide to working and healing with divinities and deities /
Doreen Virtue.
 p. cm.
Includes bibliographical references and index.
 ISBN 1-40190-018-6 (hardcover) • ISBN 1-40190-063-1 (tradepaper)
 1. Angels—Miscellanea. 2. Gods—Miscellanea. 3. Ascended masters. 4. Prayers. I. Title.
BF1999 .V586 2003
299'.93—dc21   2002014419

ISBN 13: 978-1-4019-0063-2
ISBN 10: 1-4019-0063-1

09 08 07 06   13 12 11 10
1st printing, April 2003
10th printing, May 2006

Printed in the USA

"There are those who have reached God directly, retaining no trace of worldly limits and remembering their own Identity perfectly. These might be called the Teachers of teachers because, although they're no longer visible, their image can yet be called upon. And they will appear when and where it's helpful for them to do so. To those to whom such appearances would be frightening, they give their ideas. No one can call on them in vain. Nor is there anyone of whom they're unaware. All needs are known to them, and all mistakes are recognized and overlooked by them. The time will come when this is understood. And meanwhile, they give all their gifts to the teachers of God who look to them for help. . . ."

— from *A Course in Miracles* Manual for Teachers

To God, the archangels,
and the ascended masters . . .
with eternal gratitude and
appreciation for their
Divine love, lessons, and support.

Contents

PART II: Invocations for Specific Needs and Issues

Prayers to Connect with Multiple Divinities for Specific Needs   195

PART III: A List of Whom to Call Upon for Specific Needs

APPENDIX

Gratitude

So many wonderful beings, on Earth and Heaven, collectively helped to create this book. I first want to thank Steven Farmer, my twin flame and amazing husband. My deepest appreciation to Louise L. Hay, Reid Tracy, Jill Kramer, Christy Salinas, Leon Nacson, and all of the Hay House angels. Many blessings to Bill Christy for his help with researching two of the more elusive fellows in the spirit world! Thank you to my family for being so loving, supportive, and open-minded, including Bill and Joan Hannan, Ada Montgomery, Charles Schenk, Grant Schenk, Nicole Farmer, Catherine Farmer, Susan Clark, and Nancy Fine.

Thank you to Mary Kay and John Hayden, Mairead Conlon, and Marie and Ted Doyle for bringing Steven and me to Ireland, and for providing us with the beautiful home in the midst of Marie's magical fairy glen. Thank you to Bronny Daniels, Lynnette Brown, Kevin Buck, Johnna Michelle, and Carol Michaels for your support (and the Reiki) during the writing of this book. Many blessings to Sharon George for the beautiful artwork that graces the cover.

I also want to thank those who submitted stories about their interactions with the ascended masters. And a huge bouquet of gratitude to those who read my books, use my oracle cards, listen to my audio programs, and attend my seminars. I am honored to work with you, and I appreciate your support very much.

And, as to my heavenly friends, there are no words to express my love and appreciation for the constant care and companionship you provide for me . . . for all of *us*. Thank you for guiding my words and research throughout the writing of this book.

I couldn't have done it without you all!

Introduction
From Old Age to New Age

An ascended master is a great healer, teacher, or prophet who previously walked upon the earth, and who is now in the spirit world, helping us from beyond. Ascended masters come from all cultures, religions, and civilizations, both ancient and modern. They include legendary figures such as Jesus, Moses, and Buddha; saints; goddesses and gods; and *bodhisattvas*, devas, and deities.

I've consciously worked with several specific archangels (extremely powerful angels who help us and who oversee the guardian angels) and ascended masters for many years, such as Archangel Michael, Jesus, and Mary. I've written about ascended masters and archangels in many of my books, and I've presented information about them at my workshops.

During my readings, I frequently help people understand which deities are with them as spirit guides. In fact, I first met many of the divinities (another term for "Divine beings") listed in this book during my readings. Sometimes I'll call on audience members at my workshops and ask them to stand up because I can see that they have so many ascended masters around them. I always ask people the same questions, and consistently receive the same answers:

Q: "Did you know that you have many ascended masters with you?"
A: "Yes" (or "I was hoping that I did").
Q: "Did you call these beings to your side?"
A: "Yes. I asked God to send me anyone who could help."

Even though I'd met and heard about these great beings, I wanted to acquire additional knowledge about the ancient Eastern divinities, as well as the New Age ascended masters. I wanted to get to know them firsthand, develop a personal relationship with each one, and know about each being's history and unique traits . . . instead of accepting secondhand reports about their personalities, characteristics, and functions from others.

So, in effect, I've written this book to function as a "Who's Who in the Spirit World," since, like many people I've met, I was confused about the identities, functions, and trustworthiness of the divinities I'd heard of up till now and had received conflicting reports about some of them. For example, I'd heard that some goddesses were friendly, while others were considered not-so-amicable. I'd also received mixed reports about various ascended masters associated with the New Age, and gods and goddesses of ancient cultures and Eastern religions. And then there were all of those saints and archangels!

Personal Choices

I've never felt comfortable telling people who they "should" talk to in the spirit world. Although I work closely with Jesus, I don't feel compelled to push him onto others. My role has been akin to helping people set their radio dial to whatever station they feel comfortable listening to. In my books and workshops, I teach people how to open the channels of Divine communication so they can more clearly see, hear, feel, and know the messengers of Heaven.

As such, I consider this book to be more of an *introduction* to various ascended masters. I recommend that you create your own experience with each deity to see if you feel happier, healthier, and more peaceful as a result. That is, act like a scientist: Try working with these Divine beings, and then notice the results.

Calling on ascended masters isn't the same as worshiping them—far from it! It's more like the "Phone-a-Friend" segment on the TV game show *Who Wants to Be a Millionaire.* If you're not familiar with it, on this program, contestants can call any one of five friends to help them answer a difficult question. For example, if they're asked a question about algebra, they could phone their college math professor (while simultaneously praying to God for help).

On that show, just like in life, there may be *several* people you know who are available to help you. As far as I'm concerned, the more friends who can help you, the better!

In other words, you can work with Jesus as your primary guide, yet still develop a benevolent relationship with other wonderful beings. You don't have to align yourself with a particular religious group or engage in impeccable behavior to attract the guidance and assistance of ascended masters. You only need to call upon them with a sincere heart, which you'll read more about later on.

In ancient times, many of the deities listed in this book were worshiped in the same way that many of us currently worship our Creator. Today, we don't *worship* deities—we appreciate them. They have small *g*'s in front of their *god* and *goddess* titles to show that they're aspects of *the* God with a capital *G*. The deities represent the various faces, aspects, personality variables, and unique traits that God presents to us. And ultimately, since God is omnipresent, then God is within the deities and also within us. In other words, all of the deities and all of us are *one* with God.

Just so there's no misunderstanding, this isn't a book promoting *polytheism,* which is the belief in, and worship of, many gods. As mentioned above, the deities in this book are aspects or creations of *the* God, with a capital *G*. The point that needs to be emphasized is that I'm not encouraging you to engage in the *worship* of divinities, but to *appreciate* them as gifts that our Creator has given us to help us love more, heal in all ways, and evolve on our spiritual path. When we accept their help, we're saying *thank you* to God.

The world's three major religions are *monotheistic,* a term derived from the Greek words *monos,* meaning "only," and *theos,* meaning "God." Judaism, Christianity, and Islam are monotheistic because people affiliated with these faiths believe that there's only one God. Christianity divides God into three aspects: the Father, the Son, and the Holy Spirit; however, it emphasizes that these are all aspects of the one single Creator. In the same way, the angels, archangels, and ascended masters are one with God and fit into a monotheistic system.

Monotheism is in contrast to:

- **Agnosticism:** The lack of certainty about God, gods, spirituality, or religion. Someone who practices this is unsure or uncertain about God.

- **Atheism:** Denying the existence of God or spirituality.

- **Deism:** The belief and certainty in natural religion, emphasizing morality.

- **Henotheism:** The worship of just one God, while acknowledging that other gods exist (or at least, being open to the possibility).

- **Pantheism:** The belief that everything is God, and that God is in everything and everyone.

- **Polytheism:** The belief in, and worship of, many gods, instead of a single Creator.

A Treasure Chest of History

While conducting research for this book, I consulted dozens of books; encyclopedias about saints, gods, goddesses, divinities, and archangels; and experts in the field. I also reviewed pages and pages of channeled information, using my background as a psychic psychotherapist to access helpful and authentic material about ascended masters.

Some of the New Age material I came across seemed authentic, but was so filled with esoteric lingo that I felt that it would seem unfathomable to those not familiar with such terms. For instance, who but a seasoned New Ager would know what a "Chohan of the Sixth Ray" is? Yes, this was typical of the material I found during my research of New Age ascended masters.

I wanted to create a book filled with down-to-earth explanations of the who, what, and where of each ascended master. I also wanted to provide a simple way for people to discern which divinity to call upon for specific issues. For example, I wanted to explain whom to call upon for healing, for help with abundance issues, and for relationship and family matters.

It seemed simple enough, but the task was daunting, as there are thousands of deities. This undertaking was complicated by my desire to also research ascended masters popularized by Madame Blavatsky, co-founder of the Theosophical Society, and her successors, Alice Bailey and Elizabeth Clare Prophet. Blavatsky began channeling beings whom she called "Brothers and Mahatmas" in the late 1870s and early 1880s. Blavatsky made names such as Kathumi, Serapis Bey, El Morya, and Saint-Germain famous in New Age circles.

During her stage shows, Blavatsky would "call up" disembodied voices and ghostly male figures who materialized handwritten messages. The critics of her day charged that the letters were in Blavatsky's and her staff members' handwriting and that she paid people to appear onstage in the guise of ascended masters.

In 1915, Alice Bailey, the daughter of a wealthy British aristocratic family, met Blavatsky and immersed herself in Theosophy. Alice began receiving channeled messages from Kathumi, and also a Tibetan Master named Djwhal Khul. She published 24 books stemming from these channeled messages, which are filled with profound, extremely advanced spiritual concepts.

From the 1950s to the present day, Elizabeth Clare Prophet and her late husband, Mark, repopularized interest in these beings, and added a few of their own.

Blavatsky, Bailey, and Elizabeth Clare Prophet all used exotic-sounding language such as: "The threefold flame of life," and "Elohim of the third ray," which isn't clearly defined. However, my background in psychology, philosophy, and channeling taught me to keep an open mind. I'd heard about Kathumi, El Morya, and Master Hillarion for years, and I'd listened to Elizabeth Clare Prophet's taped lectures. I'd even had my own profound experiences with Serapis Bey and Saint-Germain.

But I wondered, *Who were these figures, really?* Being a consummate researcher, I wasn't satisfied to rely solely upon the channelings of others. I wanted to know more about these masters' historical backgrounds myself, and hear about other people's experiences with them.

While researching the "new" ascended masters, I came across thousands of references from different sources—many of whom quoted Blavatsky's, Bailey's, and Elizabeth Clare Prophet's channeled words verbatim. In other words, there weren't many other sources of information about the masters. I did learn, though, that several of the ascended masters' current personas were apparently based on real people who had actually lived, and that their names were pseudonymous to protect the real person's identity. In addition, Blavatsky, Bailey, and Prophet contended that the ascended masters often had past lives as famous personas such as Pythagorus, Christopher Columbus, and Saint Francis.

I continued to look into these new ascended masters, but in some cases, I hit a brick wall. It seems that there is little information known about the history of some of the New Age ascended masters—other than what Blavatsky, Bailey, and Prophet have written about them.

However, I knew from experience that channeling is multidimensional, and even a person who is channeling her own ego may also pick up authentic and ultimately helpful material. So I tried contacting the beings myself. I figured that if they answered, there might be some cause for further investigation, which perhaps a researcher even more tenacious than myself might be willing to tackle.

So, when I contacted some of the New Age deities and was greeted with profoundly loving experiences and amazing information, I was pleasantly surprised. I've included the various "new" or New Age ascended masters primarily as a reference tool to know who's who in the spirit world. In cases where their origins are dubious, I've noted so within the pages of this book.

The New Age ascended masters aren't so different from the "Old-Age" divinities, however. Many ancient deities were based on legend and tradition rather than living humans. The Greeks and Romans, for instance, never stated that their gods and goddesses were actual people who crossed over. To them, these deities started out in the spirit world and remained there.

As I contacted each Old Age and New Age deity, I was struck by the completeness and distinctiveness of each being's personality and energy. Talking with each one was akin to having unique conversations with a wide variety of powerful men and women.

Often, I'd forestall doing the research on a deity until after I'd first contacted him or her. I was amazed by how closely my personal experiences matched the written descriptions of that deity's unique traits and characteristics. For instance, when I contacted Artemis, a powerful pixielike woman appeared to me. I later saw paintings of her that perfectly matched the way I saw her.

I was also struck by how similar the birth stories of the male deities were. Repeatedly, I read tales telling of a patriarchal figure who would issue sweeping orders to execute all the male babies in his kingdom because he was threatened by potential competition. The mother of the infant would hide her son, and the child would grow up in powerful circumstances that encouraged his spiritual knowledge and encouraged him to become a great hero.

I also read many accounts of a male deity being born to a rich or royal family, and then denying his heritage in favor of spiritual teaching and leadership. I started to realize that these stories were archetypal legends that may or may not be based upon historical fact.

Perhaps these stories—and even the deities themselves—provide a way to teach people about some aspect of God, such as the potential for His healing ability to be encased within the persona of a healing god. Or, maybe if we focus our prayers and thoughts on a concept over time—such as a goddess or god—the collective thought-forms gel into a living spiritual organism that behaves in the way we've come to expect. All of our human thought power is encapsulated into this deity, and comes back to us like principal and interest in a spiritual bank account. It's possible that we humans tap in to divinities that already exist. Or it's possible that our collective beliefs and legends "create" these beings, who then come to have a real life force of their own.

Surrounded by Love

My job with this book was clear: I was to select a few ascended masters, get to know them personally, do research on each one, channel messages from them, and then write down my experiences and recommendations. You hold the result in your hands. I apologize if I've left out your favorite ascended master. I needed to keep my list somewhat concise so as to not overwhelm you, the reader, with a multitude of deities. Through prayer and hard work, my intent was to create a book covering a wide range of divinities that would offer something for everyone.

While researching and writing this book, I had the wonderful opportunity to "hang out" with these amazingly wonderful, loving, and powerful divinities. I would often work late into the night after teaching a workshop all day long. So, my last thoughts before hitting the pillow would be about the goddess or *bodhisattva* I'd just finished writing about. During the night, I'd feel that I was surrounded by loving energy, as I would often be contacted by the divinities. I'd awaken feeling refreshed, utterly filled with Divine love!

Most of the channelings recorded in this book occurred outdoors, in fantastic natural settings. I was fortunate enough to spend time leaning against the magical rocks of Stonehenge and Avesbury in England; gazing at the mystical Irish Sea; climbing up the craggy volcanic coast of Kona, Hawaii; walking across the verdant hills of New Zealand; and stepping among the towering boulders of Joshua Tree, California, while channeling these messages.

One remarkable experience occurred during the channelings. I'd discovered that each ascended master delivered completely unique messages to me, and that each one had a distinct personality and style. Yet I was amazed that two ascended masters, Maitreya and Hotei, gave me virtually the same message word for word—both talked about the importance of joy and laughter. I'd channeled them several days apart, yet their messages seemed to be a continuation of the other, so I asked them to tell me what was going on.

A few hours later, I found myself in a shop that carried Buddhist materials. The first book that I selected opened almost automatically to a page about Hotei. Imagine my amazement when the material explained that Maitreya and Hotei *were the same beings!* I continued my investigation and found that this was correct. No wonder they'd told me the same thing!

❧ ❧ ❧ ❧

As a result of writing this book, I've discovered some ascended masters whom I didn't realize I was already working with. I've also consciously developed close relationships with some deities who are new to me. As you read along, you'll see that these relationships have been joyful and miraculous. My prayer is that you'll experience these beings as the loving friends that they are, and enjoy the powerful assistance that they offer us.

Within these pages, I also describe the ascended masters whom I consider to be highly trustworthy. These beings work closely with the Creator, our guardian angels, and all lightworkers on Earth to steer us in the direction of peace. They donate their afterlife time toward this cause, when they could be relaxing in the spirit world instead.

The divinities can also assist us with situations that may come up in the future, inspired by Earth and societal changes. They can help us avert "natural disasters," avoid or contain wars, ensure adequate food and water supplies, and heal our bodies. No matter what happens, the archangels and ascended masters will be with us. No one can take them away from us! And that's one more reason why it's wise for lightworkers to become familiar with the various divinities, and to be aware of the special gifts they offer. In the future, these Divinities will prove to be valuable allies (just as they are in the present).

The Newer Masters

There are some very powerful beings who have recently departed their physical bodies who are helping planet Earth from their home in the spirit world. A few of them are well known, while many are obscure personalities whose names you wouldn't recognize. I've come into contact with many of these "New Masters" during my readings, including Dr. Martin Luther King, Jr., Walt Disney, John Denver, and Mother Teresa.

However, I didn't include them in the body of this book because they're more along the lines of "famous spirit guides," rather than seasoned ascended masters. We can definitely call upon these great beings for help, and they will also offer assistance without our conscious realization. Several decades from now, these beings will likely move to the higher frequencies of their ascended associates.

When I was sitting next to the stones of Stonehenge, for example, the late Princess Diana began speaking to me while I was recording messages from Celtic deities. I didn't invoke her or call upon her; she came to me on her own. She mentioned right up front that she knows she wasn't considered the greatest mother, but said that her children were always of the greatest concern to her.

She then clearly said to me, *"Now the world's children are foremost on my mind. The children of the world are at a crossroads and in great need of leadership. I'm concerned for their welfare, as are you and a great many others. There is a schism with their underlying mass, as they reach for attainment of their way. The bubbling undercurrent of dissatisfaction among them is bursting into violent rage.*

"Just as my death was considered quite violent, so do I also see many outbursts by youth on the horizon that will shock us all . . . unless intervention can be reached.

"A grassroots campaign by mothers is the only solution that will lead us out of this ditch that has been created, a ditch buried with children, their parents, and their educators. This ditch is sinking deeper by the minute, and there is no time to waste.

"Many of us here have formed a committee to oversee adult volunteers who want to do something about it. Ask me to give you an assignment if you're hard-pressed to know what's expected of you in this campaign."

It's interesting that people whom I meet in North America readily see Princess Di as a benevolent spiritual helper, but the idea isn't so acceptable in Great Britain, where she was often vilified when she was alive. Regardless, I found her message quite compelling, which is why I included it here.

Ask from Love

The divinities described in this book are quite real. If you're new to working with spirit guides, or you're skeptical about their existence, you'll soon find that just *reading* this book is an invocation to the great divinities by your side. They will all come rapidly to whoever calls, without exception.

I had many powerful experiences with the divinities while writing this book. For instance, I still had about half of the deities to record invocations for after I'd finished the bulk of the book, so over a period of two days, I wrote invocations nonstop. I finished writing them the morning before a flight from Chicago's O'Hare airport into Phoenix's Sky Harbor airport—two very large, crowded places.

All that day, my husband and I kept marveling at how smoothly everything was going. For instance, the airport personnel were exceptionally nice, I had one of the best vegan meals I'd ever had on a plane, we were upgraded to a wonderful hotel room in Phoenix, and doors kept opening for us throughout the balance of the day. Steven and I noticed that we each felt wonderful, both physically and emotionally.

"What a great day this is," we kept saying to each other. "Everything's going so well!" Then we realized why: I'd invoked so many deities prior to the flight that we were being helped and guided by Heaven's cream of the crop!

�☀ �☀ ᚜ ᚜

Some advice I'd like to impart to you is this: Be sure to only ask the deities to help you with tasks associated with Divine love. If you ask them to fulfill a request involving revenge or acrimony, the negative energy will bounce back to you magnified. If you're in a situation where you're angry with someone, it's best to ask the divinities to create a peaceful solution instead of extracting a pound of flesh from the other person. After all, your true goal is always peace, and the ascended masters are very happy to manifest this for you. In fact, ascended masters help anyone who asks—regardless of that person's spiritual, religious, or lifestyle background—because they're here to enact God's plan of worldwide peace, one person at a time. Please don't worry that you're wasting the deities' time by asking for so-called small favors. If those favors bring you peace, then it's these beings' sacred honor to help you.

Besides, they're not limited to just helping one person at a time. The ascended masters can help an infinite number of people simultaneously, while having a uniquely personal experience with each individual.

The Format and Layout of This Book

This is not an all-inclusive book about deities by any means. Instead, as I mentioned earlier, I've limited my selection of ascended masters to those I've had positive experiences with. I've also whittled down the background material concerning these beings. This book doesn't tackle the entire mythological history of, for instance, the sun god Apollo. Instead, it offers enough information so that you can understand how Apollo and the other deities can become part of your spiritual team. Should you desire more background information on a particular ascended master, you can consult one of the exhaustive encyclopedias available on the subject—several of which are listed in the Bibliography.

In Part I, you'll find the most commonly used name of the divinity, alternate names, and his or her country, religion, or affiliation of origin. Then, you'll read a brief history and background about the being, followed by a current story or channeling (I've put the deities' words in *italics* to make them stand out from the rest of the text). Next, there's a list called "Helps with," outlining the specific life areas that the divinity offers assistance with.

After that, I've presented an invocation that will help you contact that particular deity. The invocations provided in this book are suggestions, not hard-and-fast rules. In fact, I like to think of them as "invitations" rather than "invocations." If you're new to working with invocations, then this book will give you a great starting point. However, in much the same way that you add your own variations to recipes while cooking, you're encouraged to use your own wording to invoke the deities. After all, the specific words that you use don't matter to the ascended masters. It's the fact that you called upon them, and that you've opened your heart in an effort to receive spiritual help.

Part II lists prayers you can use when working with multiple divinities, applicable to specific problems or situations. Just as with the invocations in Part I, these prayers are merely templates and not rigid directives. Use the words that come into your heart and mind as your guide. Then you can't go wrong when calling upon divinities. They're loving and entirely forgiving, so don't worry that eloquence is required to elicit their help!

In Part III, you'll find desired goals and life areas of all types, such as "Increasing Faith" or "Finding Soulmate Relationships." Beneath each heading are all the ascended masters and archangels who specialize in that particular area. This is a list that I've always wanted to use in my own life, and it's one of the reasons why I was guided to write this book. You'll find that it's a handy reference guide to keep nearby so you'll know whom to consult during times of need.

Part IV lists various reference materials that you may find useful, such as a Glossary of Terms, and a Bibliography for further information.

This book can also function as an oracle device. Just ask any question and allow the pages to fall open. Whatever page it opens to is the one that can provide an answer to your question.

My prayer is that this work will serve as an introduction to the Divine beings who will become your close, loving companions. May this be the beginning of many beautiful relationships with the archangels and ascended masters!

PART I

The
Archangels
&
Ascended
Masters

Abundantia
(Roman; Teutonic)

Also known as *Abundia, Habone, Fulla.*

A beautiful goddess of success, prosperity, abundance, and good fortune, Abundantia is also considered to be a protector of savings, investments, and wealth. Her image graced Roman coins in centuries past.

In Roman mythology, Abundantia brought money and grain to people while they were sleeping, shaking her gifts from the cornucopia she continuously carried.

In Norse mythology, she was called Fulla, the first and favorite attendant of Frigg (the Norse goddess of the atmosphere and clouds). Fulla carried Frigg's valuables for her, and also acted as her intermediary, performing favors for mortals who called upon the goddess for help.

Every time I see Abundantia, gold coins magically spill from her, from no particular container. The coins just seem to pour out of her, and even trail behind her, accompanied by a musical jangling sound similar to belly dancers who jingle their coin-laden outfits.

She's a vision of great beauty and angelic purity, very patient and extremely loving. *"I'm a way-shower to the mighty Source of all,"* she says. *"It's my greatest pleasure to reward your efforts, and I become ecstatic at the sound of gratitude and joy when someone is rescued through my interventions. I'm here to serve, to help you plan for uninterrupted financial bliss, and to uncover hidden treasures that you do not yet know of."*

Abundantia is like a gracious hostess, constantly asking if you need anything, and then lovingly fulfilling your every wish. She says, *"I also easily come into your dreams to answer any questions you may have about high finance, investments, and such. Never forget that finances can fuel healing projects and afford you freedom where time is concerned. But money can also be a trap if you allow worry and concern to rule over you. That's where I come in: to alleviate these lower thoughts and take you to the high road of prosperity."*

Helps with:

- Abundance, attracting all kinds of
- Financial investments, guidance about and protection of
- Good fortune
- Valuables, protecting

INVOCATION

As a show of your faith in Heaven's readiness to help you, hold one or more coins in the hand you don't write with (this is your receptive hand), and say:

"Beautiful Abundantia, I desire to be like you—carefree and filled with faith that my supply is already met in all ways. Help me replace any money worries with joy and gratitude. Help me open my arms so that Heaven may easily help me. Thank you for all of your guidance, gifts, and protection. I'm truly grateful, and I'm abundantly joyful and fulfilled. I let go, and relax in the sure knowledge that I'm completely taken care of, immediately and in the future."

Aengus
(Ireland)

Also known as *Angus, Oenghus, Angus McOg, Angus of the Brugh*.

Aengus is a Celtic god of soulmate love. His name means "young son." Aengus plays a magical golden harp that mesmerizes all who hear its sweet melodies. Like Cupid, he draws soulmates together. Whenever romance is threatened by quarrels or outside interference, Aengus weaves a net of his golden harp music around the lovers and draws them back together. It's said that when he blows a kiss, it turns into a beautiful bird who carries his romantic messages to lovers who ask for his help. Aengus lives among the fairies in a *brugh* (a fairy glen). He's the half-brother of the goddess Brigit.

Aengus's help with love relationships is legendary, beginning with his introduction to his own soulmate, Caer. Aengus first saw Caer in a dream, and his heart immediately swelled with the deepest of love for her. Upon awakening, Aengus went on a search for his beloved, although he didn't yet know who or where she was. But the determined Aengus eventually found Caer, who was bound by silver chains to beautiful swans. Aengus shape-shifted into a swan in order to successfully rescue her, and they were united in love forever.

The two soulmates sang and played romantic music to lovers everywhere. He also escorted two young lovers named Diarmuid and Grainne out of harm's way. Once they were safely ensconced, Aengus confronted their persecutor until he agreed to stop pursuing the two lovers.

It was very fitting that I first met Aengus when I called to him from my bench overlooking the Irish sea, south of Dublin. A very handsome, princely, and regal-looking man in his late 20s to mid-30s appeared to me. *"Let your servant be your master,"* he told me in a warm accent. What did this koan mean? He used it in the context of romantic love, like a key to establishing and maintaining a great relationship. He seemed to imply that this was particularly a secret for romantic dealings with men. But I still didn't know what he meant. So I sat back and meditated on the phrase.

Then, Aengus told me more: *"Never become a slave or captive to any person, substance, or situation. Be a willing servant. Give freely from a willing heart. In this way, you ensure freedom from the ensnarement of resentment, which builds up like plaque around the fond heart and extinguishes rapture. Give freely to your love, without regard for reward or consequences, but simply motivated by the pure pleasure that comes from giving . . . and that is its own reward."*

Helps with:

- Music, the romantic use of
- Passion and romance—rekindling it and keeping it alive
- Soulmate relationships—finding, creating, and protecting

INVOCATION

Wear or hold something red or pink to symbolize romance, play some soft music (preferably with harps), and call to Aengus:

"Princely Aengus, I ask for your help with my love life [describe your specific desires]. I ask for your intervention, that you may bring harmony, passion, and romance into my heart and life. I have so much love to share, and I need your help. If I'm blocking great love in some way, please help me release this block now. Thank you, Aengus."

Aeracura
(Ireland)

Aeracura is a Celtic Earth mother and Earth deity who carries a basket of fruit, or horn-of-plenty.

When I called upon her while sitting by the Irish sea, my heart immediately felt uplifted with the most lighthearted and playful type of love! I saw a beautiful fairy woman with porcelain skin and flowing light brown hair, wearing a creamy body-skimming gown that glowed. She had love in her eyes, but with a glimmer of one who enjoys a good laugh and a bit of harmless mischief in the most innocent way. She let me know that playfulness and a carefree spirit are at the heart of abundant manifestation. She emphasized this point, and I felt it in my body and heart chakra: The key to rapid and efficient manifestation is enjoyment of the process.

She said, *"I will always bring a basket of goodies to those who are receptive, mindful, and willing to receive. Think of my bountiful gifts as children who share toys with each other. It's more fun to play when you share with your friends! Call upon me for emergency money, and I shall rush to your rescue. I'm especially fond of supporting artists and nonconformists. Be not bashful in saying what you desire as you approach me. Notice how my name has a derivative of the word* cure *in it. Let's play! I love you!"*

Helps with:

- Artists and inventors, guiding and supporting
- Emergency money
- Manifestations

INVOCATION

Go outside to call upon Aeracura. Take off your shoes and socks and connect to Mother Earth with bare feet. Say to her:

"Dearest Aeracura, please come to me now. Please fill my heart with your great Divine love. Please clear my heart and mind of cares and worries. I ask that you bring your basket of bountiful gifts to me, and help me receive these gifts with love and gratitude. Help me tap in to my creativity and unleash my inner artist, to help express my love in a way that benefits the world. Please help me accept support for my artistic and creative projects."

Aine
(Ireland)

Also known as *Aine of Knockaine,* because her spirit is said to
live in a castle in Knockainy, Ireland.

Aine is an Irish moon goddess of love, fertility, protection, and environmental concerns. Her name means "bright." She's aligned with
the fairies, and is often thought of as a Fairy Queen (the equivalent of
an archangel in the elemental kingdom). There are many conflicting stories about Aine's beginnings and heritage as a goddess.

She was worshiped on Midsummer Eve with rituals where people
would hold torches over farm fields to ask Aine for help with produc-
tivity. She protects women, especially those who respect the planet's
sanctity and revere Mother Earth and her plight. She's a strong environ-
mentalist and also keenly involved in animal rights. She can clear away
curses and negative energies.

Looking like an Erté painting from a *Harper's Bazaar* magazine cover,
Aine is a lithe goddess with a distinctive art-deco look to her long, silvery
gown and pageboy hairstyle. When I spoke with her, she was poised next
to a crescent moon, surrounded by musical instruments such as harps and
pianos. Using the energy of light and musical tones, she oversees and
assists Earth and other planets in this and other solar systems.

Aine isn't here so much to help us with individual concerns, but she
says we can drape ourselves in her cloak of silver light anytime we seek
to regain our strength, and summon up the courage to speak up,

especially when performing leadership roles that will help the environment (including anything related to air and water quality, plants, and animals). Aine can help you be more playful and passionate in love relationships, as well as in your entire life. She's analogous to an archangel for the fairy and deva kingdoms—their goddess. She's especially accessible during full moons and lunar eclipses.

She says, *"I radiate Divine pure love energy like a satellite beam, positioned from the moon to divert any poisonous intentions, deeds, words, thoughts, or actions."*

Helps with:

- Animal rights and healing
- Environmental concerns
- Faith and passion, increasing
- Fertility and child conception
- Healing animals, people, and relationships
- Full-moon meditations and ceremonies
- Playfulness and enjoyment of life
- Protection, especially for women

INVOCATION

On the evening of a full moon, go outside near plants or a body of water and say aloud or mentally:

"Beloved Aine, I call upon you now. Please help me grow stronger, more powerful, and more filled with faith. Please ignite the passions of my soul, and help me relax enough to have fun and be playful while I fulfill my mission and responsibilities. Please guide me as to how I can best help the world's environment, and please surround me with loving people."

Aphrodite
(Greece)

Also known as *Cytherea, Cypris, Aphrodite Pandemos,*
Aphrodite Urania, Venus.

Aphrodite is the goddess of love, beauty, and passion, associated with the planet Venus.

Her name means "water born" or "foam born," because it's been said that she was conceived when her father, the sky god Uranus, impregnated the ocean. Her multiple love affairs with gods such as Adonis and Ares are legendary, and that's also why Aphrodite is closely associated with passionate sexuality.

She's known as both Aphrodite Urania, representing soulmate love with commitment and spirituality; and Aphrodite Pandemos, representing purely physical lust. One of her many children is Eros, a god of romantic love who in Cupid-like fashion sends arrows to those on his matchmaking list.

I spoke with Aphrodite one evening in Kona, Hawaii, when the planet Venus was high in the sky. As she came to me, I felt her before I could see her. Then I saw a woman's face enclosed in a Valentine's heart.

"I'm here to help strengthen long-term relationships, built on a dual foundation of passion and understanding," she said.

"One without the other is useless. One is for intertwining lives and bodies; the other, for talks and discussions. Even still, there is much overlap, for

a lover who understands your needs and desires is a great lover indeed. And a partner who holds passion in the heart toward you will be motivated to heal occasional hurts and wounds, and be captivated long enough to attain an understanding.

"The nature of the ever-growing, ever-living relationship is one that always thirsts after more passion and more knowledge within the context of commitment."

Helps with:

- Commitment, engagements, and marriage
- Femininity, gracefulness, beauty, and attraction/attractiveness
- Sexuality, including increasing desire and romantic passion

INVOCATION

Put yourself in a receptive mood, perhaps by listening to romantic music, watching a movie about lovers, dressing seductively, or holding a rose. Then, focus on your heart and say aloud or mentally:

"Aphrodite, I'm open to being loved deeply and completely in a romantic relationship. Please help me release any remaining blocks that could delay this manifestation. I ask that you help me radiate my inner light, and attract great love now. Please help me fully enjoy this love, and to know that I deserve it."

Apollo
(Greece)

A pollo is a sun god who oversees prophecy, light, music, and healing.

Apollo is one of the original 12 Olympian gods and goddesses. He's the son of Zeus and twin brother of the goddess Artemis. Apollo had many lovers and dozens of offspring. Legends abound about Apollo's birth family and life. One of his most famous children is Asclepius, the legendary god of healing and medicine, for whom hospitals are named after.

Apollo has always willingly offered his help to humans who need it, and he continues to intervene where needed today. He spent much time in ancient Delphi, helping oracles and prophets with their divinations. Today he helps psychics and spiritual mediums elevate their gifts to the highest of spiritual frequencies. In New Age circles, Apollo is known as an *Elohim* (which in Hebrew means "divinities"), who bestows Divine wisdom and spiritual understanding upon Earth and her inhabitants.

Apollo heals physical and emotional wounds and awakens psychic gifts by helping to replace unforgiveness with compassion and understanding. He's extremely handsome, with a lean and golden muscular form that radiates youthful beauty. Apollo motivates us to take excellent care of our bodies, and to make physical fitness an intricate part of our lifestyle.

He says, *"I am the sun god—invoke me for light of any type: Divine, mechanical, radiant, healing, or a sunshiny day. I now exist in all dimensions, so I'm available to respond to all levels of concerns. I infuse your planet with light, even on the dreariest of days."*

Helps with:

- Exercise and healthful eating; increasing motivation
- Happy endings to stressful situations
- Mechanical problems, fixing
- Psychic, clairvoyant, and prophetic abilities—opening and polishing
- Weather—banishing clouds in favor of sunshine, both literally and metaphorically

INVOCATION

Wear or hold something golden or yellow (like the sunlight associated with Apollo), and play lively music. Apollo can be contacted anytime you need assistance; however, you may have the best connection at high noon when the sun is at its peak. Say to Apollo:

"Brightest of the bright, Apollo, please come to me now. Please shine light upon me so that I may see it clearly. Help me gain a deeper understanding of my situation so that I and everyone involved may be healed. Help me feel compassion for myself and others, and to release any anger or unforgiveness now. Please help me lose all heaviness in my body, mind, and heart so that I may soar high like you."

Archangel Ariel
(Cabalistic)

Also known as *Arael, Ariael.*

Ariel's name means "lion or lioness of God," and this archangel, predictably, is often associated with lions. When Ariel is near, you might begin seeing references to, or visions of, lions around you. In fact, some artwork portrays Ariel as having a lion's head. This archangel is also associated with the wind, so when Ariel is around, you may feel or hear the wind as a sign.

Archangel Ariel is described in books of Judaic mysticism and cabalistic magic, such as *The Testament of Solomon, The Greater Key of Solomon, Ezra,* and *The Hierarchy of the Blessed Angels.* Ariel works closely with King Solomon in conducting manifestation, spirit releasement (similar to exorcism), and Divine magic.

Ariel also oversees the sprites, the nature angels associated with water. Sprites are similar to fairies, and their purpose is to maintain healthy environments near oceans, lakes, rivers, streams, and ponds. Archangel Ariel may contact you to help with this mission of purifying and protecting these water bodies and their inhabitants. If you help with Ariel's environmental mission, you may be rewarded with wonderful manifestations and increased magical power.

Ariel is very involved with healing and protecting nature—and that definitely includes animals, fish, and birds—especially wild ones. If you find an injured bird or other nondomesticated animal who needs healing, call upon Ariel for help. Ariel works with Archangel Raphael to heal animals in need.

Archangel Ariel says, *"I'm deeply concerned about the world's environmental systems, which are always in delicate balance and are now in need of reform and restoration. I have plenty of assignments available for those willing to assist in this endeavor. I promise to only give out assignments that are related to your interests and time schedules. Your reward will be the joy that stretches out from your heart, extending into the very environment you're blessing with your dedicated efforts. I thank you very much for coming to the planet's rescue!"*

Helps with:

- Divine magic
- Environmentalism, especially concerning water bodies
- Manifestation
- Wild animals, fish, and birds—healing and protecting

INVOCATION

Call upon Archangel Ariel anytime, anywhere. However, you'll be most likely to feel, hear, see, and know her presence if you conduct this invocation outside in nature (especially near a body of water):

"Archangel Ariel, I call upon your presence now. I desire to help heal the world's environment, and I ask you to give me a Divine assignment for this important mission. I ask that you open the way and support me in this endeavor. Thank you for the joy that this mission brings to me and the world."

Archangel Azrael
(Hebrew, Muslim)

Also known as *Azrail, Ashriel, Azriel, Azaril, The Angel of Death.*

Azrael's name means "whom God helps." His role is primarily to help people cross over to Heaven at the time of physical death. Azrael comforts people prior to their physical passing, makes sure they don't suffer during death, and helps them assimilate on the other side. He also surrounds grieving family members with healing energy and Divine light to help them cope and thrive. Azrael lends support to surviving friends and family members, easing their journey in material, spiritual, and emotional ways. If you've lost someone, call upon Azrael for support and comfort.

Azrael also works with grief counselors to shield them from absorbing their clients' pain, and to guide their words and actions for maximum effectiveness. Call upon Azrael to bring comfort to a dying loved one, and to help during the time of crossing over. Azrael will be there for everyone concerned. You can also ask Azrael to help your departed loved one, and to meet with him or her in Heaven.

Archangel Azrael is very quiet and composed. He has great respect for the grieving process, and he doesn't impose upon those who are going through it. Moreover, Azrael stands by as a source of quiet strength and comfort.

He says, *"During sleepless nights of anxious grieving, where you toss and turn, I can ease your restless mind and help you sleep. A rested mind and body is stronger and more able to withstand the grieving process. So, do not hesitate to call on me for my prayers, assistance, or intercession during times of need. I will invoke other angels alongside you and your loved ones, and we will do everything within God's power to support you with dynamic love."*

Helps with:

- Comforting the dying and the grieving
- Crossing over the newly deceased person's soul
- Grief counseling
- Support for the grieving—material, spiritual, and emotional

INVOCATION

No special attire or behavior is necessary to call upon Archangel Azrael—just a sincere desire to help in a situation involving grief or death. Just think the thought, and Azrael is there. A sample invocation is:

"Archangel Azrael, please comfort me now. Please help me to heal. Please lift my heart above heaviness and help me realize the blessings that this situation holds. Please help me release my tears and connect to my beloved in Heaven. I ask that you infuse this connection with energy so that I may clearly communicate with [him or her]. I know that my loved one is nearby and that you watch over both of us. [If there is any situation related to the grief that you need help with, tell Azrael about it now.] Thank you, Azrael."

Archangel Chamuel
(Judeo-Christian)

Also known as *Camael, Camiel, Camiul, Camniel, Cancel,*
Jahoel, Kemuel, Khamael, Seraphiel, Shemuel.

Chamuel's name means "he who sees God," or "he who seeks God." Chamuel is usually on the list of the seven core archangels, and he's considered a powerful leader in the angelic hierarchy known as the "Powers." The Powers are angels who oversee protection of the world from fearful and lower energies. They act like bouncers who turn away anyone who would attempt to overtake the world in a negative way. If you're fearful about world events, call upon Chamuel for comfort, protection, and intervention.

Chamuel also protects our personal world, too. He helps us seek out important parts of our lives, such as love relationships, friends, careers, lost items, and our life purpose. Chamuel works with us to build strong foundations for our relationships and careers so that they're long-lasting, meaningful, and healthy.

Archangel Chamuel is very kind, loving, and sweet. You'll know he's with you when you feel butterflies in your stomach and a pleasant tingling in your body. He says, *"Allow me to escort you through life's traverses, and to make your journey smooth and successful. It's my greatest pleasure to bring in peacefulness to replace any energy of pain."*

Helps with:

- Career, life purpose, and lost items—finding
- Relationships, building and strengthening
- Soulmates, seeking out
- World peace

INVOCATION

Call upon Chamuel to recover anything that seems to be lost. He hears your thoughts, so you can mentally call him, even in when you're in a panic:

"Archangel Chamuel, I seem to have lost [name of object or situation]. I know that nothing is truly lost, since God is every-where, and therefore, can see where everything is. Please guide me to find what I'm looking for. Thank you, Chamuel."

Archangel Gabriel
(Judeo-Christian, Muslim)

Also known as *Abruel, Jibril, Jiburili, Serafili.*

Gabriel's name means "God is my strength." Gabriel (who is female) is the famous angel who told Elizabeth and Mary of the impending births of their sons, John the Baptist and Jesus of Nazareth, respectively. The Archangel Gabriel also dictated the spiritual text of Islam, The Koran, to Mohammed. As a result, Gabriel became known as the "messenger" angel. Gabriel's role continues in the world, helping both parents and human messengers.

In the first role, Gabriel guides hopeful parents toward child conception or through the process of adopting a child. Gabriel gives strength and courage to these parents, and helps moms-to-be stay centered in blissful faith to create the best atmosphere for their baby.

In the second role, the archangel helps anyone whose life purpose involves art or communication. Call upon Gabriel for help, guidance, and agenting if you're an actor, artist, author, dancer, journalist, model, musician, reporter, singer, songwriter, teacher, or do anything involving delivering spiritual messages. Gabriel will open doors to help you express your talent in a big way. The archangel also acts as a coach, inspiring and motivating artists and communicators, and helping them to overcome fear and procrastination.

Gabriel has long been known as a powerful and strong archangel, and those who call upon her will find themselves pushed into action that leads to beneficial results. Gabriel is definitely an archangel of action! She says, *"I'm here to manage those who speak up and speak out on behalf of societal needs. This process of advocacy is an ancient one, and few things have changed over the course of time, save for some technological advances. In other arenas, though, art and speech have maintained a constant and steady force, lending power to people who desire change and helpfulness. Allow me to open the doors of opportunity for those among you hearing your heart's call to perform, play, and create on a wider scale."*

Helps with:

- Adopting a child
- Artists and art-related projects
- Child conception and fertility
- Journalism and writing
- Television and radio work

INVOCATION

Before beginning any artistic or communication project, ask Gabriel to guide and oversee your activities by saying aloud or mentally:

"Archangel Gabriel, I ask for your presence as I [describe the project]. Please open my creative channels so that I may be truly inspired. Help me open my mind so that I may give birth to unique ideas. And please help me to sustain the energy and motivation to follow through on this inspiration. Thank you, Gabriel."

Archangel Haniel
(Babylonian, Cabalistic)

Also known as *Anael, Aniel, Hamiel, Onoel.*

Haniel's name means "glory of God," or "grace of God." In ancient Babylon, a group of men known as "priests-astronomers" worked with astrology, astronomy, moon energy, and various deities for their divination and spiritual healing work. One of the archangels with whom they worked was Haniel, who was associated with the planet Venus.

Some Cabalistic texts credit Haniel as escorting Enoch to the spirit world. Enoch was one of only two humans to ever be transformed into archangels—in his case, into the Archangel Metatron. (The other case was the prophet Elijah ascending into the Archangel Sandalphon, as you'll read about later on.)

Haniel helps us recover the lost secrets of natural healing remedies, especially involving the harnessing of the moon's energy in potions, powders, and crystals. Haniel also helps us enjoy more grace in our lives. To add beauty, harmony, and the company of wonderful friends to your life, call upon Haniel. This archangel will also help you stay poised and centered before and during any important event, such as a speech, performance, first date, or job interview.

Archangel Haniel has a moon goddess energy: etheric, quiet, patient, and mystical. Haniel's wisdom comes from many eons of experience in working with humans. She says, *"Yes, I'm patient with humanity because I can see all the good they've created. For every moment of intolerance, there are hundreds of deep kindnesses to overshadow the darkness. The light of humanity shines brighter today than ever. If you could see humanity from my point of view, you'd know why I have such deep regard and love for you all. I'm happy to help in whatever cause advances humanity above the din of clashing egos, and elevates you to the level from which you have come: God's grace and eternal beauty."*

Helps with:

- Grace, bringing it into our lives
- Healing abilities
- Moon energy
- Poise
- Psychic abilities, especially clairvoyance

INVOCATION

If you've got an important function coming up that demands an excellent performance or refined social graces, ask Haniel to accompany you. You can call upon Haniel by thinking her name and describing your need, or by stating a formal invocation such as:

"Archangel Haniel, overseer of grace, poise, and charm, please bring your Divine energy of loving wisdom to [describe the situation]. Thank you for guiding my words, actions, and mannerisms and helping me to enjoy myself, while bringing blessings to everyone who sees or hears me. I ask that your Divine magnetism draw only positive energies to me. O thank you, glorious Haniel, thank you."

Archangel Jeremiel
(Judaic)

Also known as *Ramiel, Remiel.*

Jeremiel's name means "mercy of God." In ancient Judaic texts, Jeremiel is listed as one of the seven core archangels.

He's also associated with helping Baruch, a prolific author of apocryphal Judaic texts in the first century A.D., with his prophetic visions. One vision, catalyzed by Jeremiel, was of the coming Messiah. In another vision, Jeremiel took Baruch for a tour of the different levels of Heaven.

In addition to being an Archangel of prophetic visions, Jeremiel helps newly crossed-over souls review their lives. This is a service he helps the still-living with, too. If you'd like to take an inventory of your life up till now so that you can make positive adjustments, call upon Jeremiel. He will help you fearlessly assess your history and learn from prior experiences so that you're even stronger and more centered in love in the future.

Jeremiel says, *"A life review today, held at regular intervals, will prove to be of great benefit to you in determining your next station and steps. By reviewing your life along the way, you make your duty that much more enjoyable when you get to the other side. You'll already have reviewed the major crossroads, and won't suffer or have regrets when you admit to yourself that you could have done better.*

"A life review is far more comprehensive on the other side, of course, but you can compose one while you're still in physicality. Carve out some quiet time and ask me to enter your thoughts or dreams at night. I shall display pictures of major events within your life that will spark your memory of smaller occurrences. It's often in those seemingly minor interactions with other people that your greatest realizations occur. This is where life lessons often spring from. Then, you can easily base your philosophies and decisions upon what you've realized, which will always be for the benefit of everyone involved."

Helps with:

- Clairvoyance and prophetic visions
- Life reviews and making life changes
- Psychic dreams, including their interpretations

INVOCATION

If you're concerned about the future, call upon Jeremiel for additional insight and information:

"Archangel Jeremiel, please help me release fears, worries, and tension about my future . . . and the future of the world. [Tell Jeremiel about any situation that is weighing particularly on your mind.] I ask for your prophetic insights about the future. Please clearly give me guidance about anything that I may do or change to create the highest and best future for myself and all concerned. Thank you."

Archangel Jophiel
(Judeo-Christian)

Also known as *Iofiel, Iophiel, Jofiel, Zophiel.*

Jophiel's name means "beauty of God." This archangel is known as "the Patron of Artists." She was present in the Garden of Eden, and later, she watched over Noah's sons.

As the archangel of art and beauty, Jophiel helps us metaphysically and physically. First, Jophiel helps us think beautiful thoughts; to see and appreciate beauty around us; and to, therefore, create, manifest, and attract more beauty into our lives. After all, beautiful thoughts lead to beautiful outcomes.

In the physical world, Jophiel helps with artistic projects and illuminates our creative spark. She gives us ideas and the energy to carry out artistic ventures. Jophiel also helps us create beauty at home, at work, and in our relationships. She helps us to slow down and smell the roses.

Archangel Jophiel has an uplifting energy that's fun and pleasant to be around. She's friendly and positive, like an ideal best friend. She says, *"Worry never helped anything, so why turn to it during times of need? It won't nurture or heal you—quite the opposite, actually. It's so much better to put the effort into something creative as a way to quietly meditate through positive action. Create, create, create! In this way, you mirror God's own creativity. That's why you feel closest to God when you're fully engaged in writing, speaking, and other artistic projects."*

Helps with:

- Artistic projects and artists
- Beautiful thoughts
- Interior decorating
- Slowing down from a hectic pace

INVOCATION

If you find yourself in an ugly situation, chances are good that ugly thoughts helped to manifest it. Call upon Jophiel to turn things around:

"Archangel Jophiel, please help me with [describe the situation]. Thank you for helping me see the inner Divine beauty within myself and everyone involved. Thank you for your intervention in creating a beautiful outcome. In gratitude, and in the name of all that is beautiful, I thank you, Jophiel."

Archangel Metatron
(Judaic, Cabalistic)

Also known as *Metatetron, Merraton, Metaraon, Mittron.*

The meaning of Metatron's name isn't clear, since his name doesn't end in the "el" suffix of all the other archangels (with the exception of Metatron's twin brother, Sandalphon). "El" stands for "El Elyah," the Hebrew name of the all-loving God of Abraham—as opposed to the jealous, vengeful God of Moses, who is called Jehovah. So, archangel names describe their function, and then end in "el" to mean "of God." The term *angel* itself means "messenger of God."

Metatron's unusual name probably stems from his uncommon origins, as one of only two archangels who were once mortal men who walked upon the earth (the other one being Sandalphon, who was the prophet Elijah). There is various speculation among texts and experts that the name Metatron means "he who occupies the throne next to the Divine throne," or that his name is a derivation of the name *Yahweh,* the Jewish term for the unspoken sacred name of God. He has also been called "the Angel of the Presence."

Metatron is the youngest of the archangels, since his creation occurred after the other archangels. The prophet and scribe Enoch, who is said to have "walked with God" (in the book of Genesis), retained his God-given purity during his mortal life. Enoch was also a scholar on heavenly secrets, having received *The Book of the Angel Raziel* (also known as *Sefer Raziel*), a textbook about God's workings penned by Archangel Raziel, and given to Adam, Noah, Enoch, and Solomon. As a result, God escorted Enoch directly to the seventh Heaven—the highest level—to reside and work. Enoch was given wings and transformed into a great archangel named Metatron.

Since Enoch was a skilled and honest scribe upon Earth, he was given a similar job in Heaven: to record everything that happened on Earth and keep it in the Akashic records (also known as *The Book of Life*). Enoch is in charge of recording and organizing this material.

Metatron is a fiery, energetic angel who works tirelessly to help Earth's inhabitants. He acts as an intermediary between Heaven and Earth, since he's had extensive experience as both a human and an angel. As such, he helps us understand Heaven's perspective, and to learn how to work with the angelic realm.

Metatron also has a special place in his heart for children, especially those who are spiritually gifted. After the Exodus, Metatron led the children of Israel through the wilderness and into safety. He continues to lead children today, both on Earth and in Heaven. Metatron is very concerned about children who are labeled as having Attention Deficit Disorder (ADD) or Attention Deficit Hyperactivity Disorder (ADHD), and he helps parents, educators, scientists, and health-care professionals find natural alternatives to Ritalin and other psychoactive medications.

Metatron helps newly crossed-over children adjust to Heaven, and helps living children love themselves and be more focused. Metatron also helps children become spiritually aware and to accept and polish their spiritual gifts.

Metatron's energy is strong and highly focused, like a laser beam. He's very motivational, and will encourage you to overcome procrastination and to take bold steps forward. He's also philosophical and can help you understand things like other people's motivations for action, and why different situations occur.

He says: *"My human life gave me the ability to grasp human concepts of life and death, which are abstract concepts to those who've always existed in the ethers. I do understand the gripping fear of death that underlies many human emotions. Having crossed that divide, though, I want to underscore the sentiment that you've so often heard: that there truly is nothing to fear in coming here. The time is planned according to your soul's calendar, and death cannot occur one moment before that time is reached.*

"There is no such thing as a premature or unplanned death, and unpleasantries associated with death are largely of the human imagination. Even those who die violently are spared from heinous suffering mainly due to God's intervention. Their souls are cast out of their bodies at the time of inevitability, long before any suffering could set in. Their disassociation with the event occurs because they're already focused upon the realization of that which follows after the physical existence. The fascination they have in experiencing their newfound life, following death, removes all concentration from the suffering that the human seems to undergo at the moment of death. We assure you that all of this comes from the compassion of the Great Creator, who is with us all, always."

Helps with:

- Attention Deficit Disorder (ADD) or Attention Deficit Hyperactivity Disorder (ADHD)
- Children's issues
- Recordkeeping and organization
- Spiritual understanding
- Writing

INVOCATION

If a child you care about has been labeled as having ADD or ADHD, and medication has been recommended or prescribed, call upon Archangel Metatron to see if alternative treatments are viable:

"Archangel Metatron, I ask for your powerfully loving intervention in helping [name of child], who has been labeled as 'disordered.' Please help us to know God's will for this child, and guide all of the adults involved to do what's best for the child. Please help us stand strong among authority figures, and to do what we know is right. Please help all of the adults involved in making decisions on behalf of this child engage in harmonious discussions, even if there are differing opinions. Metatron, please protect this child from any harm, now and in the future. Thank you."

Archangel Michael
(Judeo-Christian, Islamic)

Also known as *Beshter, Mika'il, Sabbathiel, Saint Michael.*

Michael's name means "he who is like God" or "he who looks like God." Archangel Michael is a leader among archangels. He's in charge of the order of angels known as "the Virtues," and he oversees the lightworker's life purpose. His chief function is to rid the earth and its inhabitants of the toxins associated with fear. The humans whom he enlists and works with are called "lightworkers," and Michael asks them to perform spiritual teaching and healing work on a professional or casual basis.

Michael has inspired leaders and lightworkers since his time in the Garden of Eden, where he taught Adam how to farm and care for his family. Joan of Arc told her inquisitors that it was the Archangel Michael who gave her the impetus and courage to lead France during the Hundred Years' War. In 1950, he was canonized as Saint Michael, "the Patron of Police Officers," because he helps with heroic deeds and bravery.

Archangel Michael is extremely tall and handsome, and he usually carries a sword, which he uses to release us from the snare of fear. When he's around, you may see sparkles or flashes of bright blue or purple light. Michael is a fiery energy, and his presence is enough to make you sweat. I've had a number of female students tell me that they thought they were having menopausal hot flashes until they realized they'd just invoked Michael, and it was his presence creating all the heat!

Michael also has an incredible knack for fixing electrical and mechanical devices, including computers. I've called on him a number of times to help me with errant telephones, fax machines, and types of electronics, and he always comes through. A student of mine even invoked him when she was fixing a friend's plumbing (something she knew nothing about, but offered to do because she had faith that she *could* figure it out). As soon as this woman called Michael, the plumbing seemed to fix itself, and the operation was completed in no time!

Michael guides and directs those who feel lost, or stuck with respect to their life's purpose or career path. He can stimulate the unmotivated or fearful into action. Michael also provides clear guidance about which step to take next.

Helps with:

- Commitment and dedication to one's beliefs
- Courage
- Direction
- Energy and vitality
- Life's purpose, all aspects of
- Motivation
- Protection
- Space clearing
- Spirit releasement
- Worthiness and increased self-esteem

INVOCATION

Call upon Michael whenever you feel afraid or vulnerable. He will instantly come to your side, lending you courage and ensuring your safety, both physically and emotionally. You'll feel his warrior-like presence next to you in much the same way that a loving bodyguard would protect you. Anyone who might have intended to harm you will have a change of mind or heart.

Michael doesn't require that you say a formal invocation, and he will come to anyone who calls upon him. For example, you could think the thought:

> "Archangel Michael, please come to me now. I need your help!"

Then mentally describe the situation with which you need assistance. As stated earlier, you'll know he's with you when you sense his characteristic warm energy.

Archangel Raguel
(Judeo-Christian)

Also known as *Akrasiel, Raguil, Rasuil, Rufael, Suryan.*

Raguel's name means "friend of God." His chief role in Heaven is to oversee all of the other archangels and angels. He ensures that they're all working well together in a harmonious and orderly fashion, according to Divine order and will. As a result, he's often referred to as "the Archangel of Justice and Fairness." Raguel loves to be a champion to underdogs, and he can help those who feel slighted or mistreated become more empowered and respected.

Archangel Raguel is enthusiastic and friendly, and he's a "battery"—meaning that he'll energize you when you need a boost. Think of having a best friend who's a combination attorney, spiritual counselor, therapist, and motivational coach, and you'll have an idea of Raguel's multiple talents and the extent of his helpfulness. Raguel is a loving gentleman who will never interfere with your free will. However, if you ask him for help, he'll be there in an instant.

He says: *"I so often see people who let themselves down without realizing their potential and options. My availability is unlimited, and there really aren't any reasons to attempt anything alone with so much friendship available. I often work anonymously within groups of other helpers, so you may not know that I'm there helping you at your request. But know that I am!"*

Helps with:

- Arguments, resolving
- Cooperation and harmony in groups and families
- Defending the unfairly treated
- Empowerment, especially for underdogs
- Mediation of disputes
- Orderliness

INVOCATION

Raguel is a wonderful resolver of conflicts. If you've had an argument with someone and you need closure with that person, ask Raguel to intervene:

"Archangel Raguel, thank you for intervening into my relationship with [name of other person involved], bringing both of us to a level of peace and harmony. I'm grateful for your help in resolving our differences with love and cooperation. I appreciate the forgiveness that we feel toward one another. I know that God's will is eternal peace, and as children of God, I'm aware that both of us are the embodiment of that peace. Thank you for helping us live that truth, now and forever. In peace and gratitude, I thank you."

Archangel Raphael
(Judeo-Christian)

Also known as *Labbiel.*

Raphael's name means "God heals" or "God has healed," based upon the Hebrew word *rapha,* which means "doctor" or "healer."

Raphael is a powerful healer of physical bodies, both for humans and animals. Those who call on Raphael are healed rapidly. It's said that he healed the pain that Abraham felt after being circumcised as an adult.

Raphael can be invoked on behalf of someone else. Raphael will go to wherever he's requested; however, he can't interfere with that person's free will. If an ailing person refuses spiritual treatment, it can't be forced. However, Raphael's presence will have a comforting effect, which will aid in natural healing by reducing stress and anxiety.

In the *Book of Tobit,* Raphael travels with Tobias, who is Tobit's son. During this journey, Raphael keeps Tobias safe from harm. This earned Raphael his other role as "the Patron of Travelers." Raphael is a wonderful aide when it comes to safe travel, assuring that all of the transportation, lodging, and luggage details go miraculously well. He also helps those on inward spiritual journeys, assisting them in their search for truth and guidance.

Raphael also showed Tobias how to use parts of the fish he'd caught in medicinal ways, such as for healing balms and ointments. This is an example of how Raphael not only conducts spiritual healing work directly upon the ill or injured, but also guides human healers in knowing which Earthly treatments to use on their patients. Healers can mentally call upon Raphael for guidance before or during treatment sessions. Raphael also helps would-be healers with their education (including getting the time and money for school), and then assists them in establishing their healing practices by attracting wonderful clients.

Raphael is a healer and guide for wild and domesticated animals. I've had wonderful results when asking Raphael to retrieve lost pets for myself, friends, and clients. The results are almost immediate, as animals seem to be especially open to his gentle, loving care.

Raphael ultimately helped heal Tobit's blindness, and he's worked with thousands of my students at my workshops to open their "third eye," which is a spiritual energy center (chakra) that regulates clairvoyance. Raphael is very sweet, loving, kind, and gentle, and you know that he's around when you see sparkles or flashes of emerald-green light.

Archangels Raphael and Michael often work in tandem to exorcise troublesome spirits and escort away lower energies from people and places. *The Testament of Solomon* describes how Raphael brought the magical ring to King Solomon, inscribed with the powerful six-pointed star. Solomon used the ring and its symbol to subdue demons. So, part of Raphael's healing work involves spirit releasement and space clearing.

Helps with:

- Addictions and cravings, eliminating and reducing
- Clairvoyance
- Eyesight, physical and spiritual
- Healers, guidance and support for
- Healing, for humans and animals
- Pets, retrieving lost
- Space clearing
- Spirit releasement
- Travelers—relating to protection, orderliness, and harmony

Invocation

Anytime that you, or another person or animal, experience physical distress, call upon Archangel Raphael for angelic treatment. He'll intervene directly into the person or animal's body, and also provide guidance about what can be done to effect a healing.

To invoke Raphael for yourself, just think to yourself:

"Archangel Raphael, I need help with [describe the situation]. Please surround and infuse my body with your powerful healing energy of Divine love. I now surrender this situation entirely to God, and know that through this releasement, I'm open to revealing my God-given health in all ways. Thank you for the energy, wellness, and happiness, God and Raphael!"

To invoke Raphael for someone else, you can visualize him and other angels surrounding that person or animal with their healing presence and emerald green light. You can ask God to send Raphael, or you can ask Raphael directly:

"Archangel Raphael, please pay a healing visit to [name of person or animal] and promote health and wellness for everyone concerned. Please help lift all of our thoughts to those of faith and hope, and remove all doubts and fears. Please clear the way so that Divine health is manifested now and forever. Thank you."

Archangel Raziel
(Judaic, Cabalistic)

Also known as *Ratziel, Saraqael, Suriel.*

Raziel's name means "secret of God" because he works so closely with the Creator that he knows all of the secrets of the Universe and how it operates. Raziel wrote down all of these secrets in a tome of symbols and Divine magic called *The Book of the Angel Raziel,* or *Sefer Raziel.* After Adam and Eve were expelled from Eden, Raziel gave Adam the book for guidance about manifestation and God's grace. Later, the prophet Enoch received the book prior to his ascension and transformation into Archangel Metatron. Noah was also given a copy of the book by Archangel Raphael, and Noah used the information to build his ark and help its inhabitants after the flood.

Many scholars say that the cryptical book (which is available today in bookstores) was actually penned by a Jewish scholar of the middle ages, perhaps Eleazar of Worms or Isaac the Blind. However, the book is difficult to decipher, and it's said that readers must call upon Raziel in order to make sense of it.

Raziel can help you understand esoteric material, manifestation principles, sacred geometry, quantum physics, and other high-level information. He can also open you up to higher levels of psychic abilities and increase your ability to see, hear, know, and feel Divine guidance. Like a Divine wizard, Raziel can also assist you with manifestations.

Raziel is very loving, kind, and intelligent. His presence can seem subtle, but as you invoke him over time, you'll become aware of his positive influence in your spiritual practices.

Helps with:

- Alchemy
- Clairvoyance
- Divine magic
- Esoteric information
- Manifestation
- Psychic abilities

INVOCATION

To deepen your spiritual understanding of esoteric concepts, call upon Raziel. Since his messages are profound, it's best to contact him in a quiet environment. Close your eyes, breathe deeply, quiet your mind, and mentally say:

"Archangel Raziel, please help me open my mind to the Divine secrets of the Universe. Help me release any limiting beliefs or fears so that I may have spiritual understanding at the deepest and clearest level. In particular, I would like your instruction about [describe a problem that you'd like a solution to, asking any questions one at a time and giving plenty of time between them so that Raziel has a chance to answer each one and you have a chance to absorb and digest his responses]. Thank you, Raziel, for teaching me."

Archangel Sandalphon
(Judaic)

Also known as *Sandolphon, Sandolfon.*

Sandalphon is only one of two archangels whose name doesn't end with an "el" (which means "God" in Hebrew). Sandalphon's name means "brother" in Greek, a reference to his twin brother, the Archangel Metatron. The twins are the only archangels in Heaven who were originally mortal men. Sandalphon was the prophet Elijah, and Metatron was the wise man Enoch. God gave both men their immortal assignments as archangels to reward them for their good work upon Earth, allowing them to continue their sacred service from Heaven. Elijah's ascension occurred when he was lifted up to Heaven in a fiery chariot pulled by two horses of fire, accompanied by a whirlwind, an event recorded in the second chapter of the Book of 2 Kings.

Sandalphon's chief role is to carry human prayers to God so they may be answered. He's said to be so tall that he extends from Earth to Heaven. Ancient Cabalistic lore says that Sandalphon can help expectant parents determine the gender of their forthcoming child, and many also believe that he's involved with music as well.

Archangel Sandalphon's messages and musings come as soft whispers on the wings of angels—they're so gentle that they can breeze by if you're not paying attention. When you invoke Sandalphon, stay aware of any words or music you hear in your mind, as they're most likely answers to your prayers.

Helps with:

- Music
- Prayers, delivering and answering
- Unborn babies, determining the gender of

INVOCATION

If you have a prayer that you urgently want answered, call upon Archangel Sandalphon by thinking of your prayer and saying:

"Beloved Archangel Sandalphon, deliverer and answerer of all prayers, I ask for your assistance now. Please deliver my prayer [recite the prayer] to God as soon as possible. I ask that you relay a clear message to me that I'll easily understand. Please update me as to the progress of my request, and let me know if I need to do anything. Thank you, and amen."

Archangel Uriel
(Judeo-Christian)

Uriel's name means "God is light," "God's light," or "fire of God," because he illuminates situations and gives prophetic information and warnings. For example, Uriel warned Noah of the impending flood, helped the prophet Ezra to interpret mystical predictions about the forthcoming Messiah, and delivered the Cabala to humankind. Uriel has also been credited with bringing the knowledge and practice of alchemy—the ability to turn base metal into precious metal, as well as the ability to manifest from thin air—to humankind.

Uriel is regarded as one of the wisest archangels. He's very much like an old sage whom you can call upon for intellectual information, practical solutions, and creative insight. Instead of having to climb a mountain to reach the sage, Uriel will instantly come to you. However, Uriel's personality isn't as distinctive as Archangel Michael's, for example. You may not even realize that Uriel has come to answer your prayers until you notice a brilliant new idea that's entered your mind.

Perhaps because of his connection to Noah, as well as his affinity with the weather elements of thunder and lightning, Uriel is considered to be an archangel who helps us with earthquakes, floods, fires, hurricanes, tornadoes, natural disasters, and Earth changes. Call upon Archangel Uriel to avert such events, or to heal and recover in their aftermath.

Helps with:

- Alchemy
- Divine magic
- Earth changes
- Problem solving
- Spiritual understanding
- Studies, tests, and students
- Weather
- Writing

INVOCATION

Since Uriel has so many talents and helps us in so many life areas, it's a good idea to call upon him regularly. Think of him as a mentor who can oversee life lessons. One of the greatest ways in which Uriel helps us is by giving us additional information so that we can make informed decisions. In such cases, call upon him in a way such as this:

"Archangel Uriel, I ask for your wisdom on [describe the situation you'd like illumination about]. I need as much information as possible so that I can clearly see the truth of the situation. Please help me make an informed decision by filling me in on all of the perspectives involved. Please help me clearly hear and understand this information, and to be as open-minded as possible. Thank you, Uriel."

Archangel Zadkiel
(Judaic)

Also known as *Satqiel, Tzadkiel, Zadakiel, Zidekiel.*

Zadkiel's name means "the righteousness of God." He's considered to be the archangel of mercy and benevolence, perhaps because of his role in stopping Abraham from sacrificing his son, Isaac, as an offering to God.

Zadkiel can help you feel mercy and compassion toward yourself and others, and let go of judgment and unforgiveness. In this way, he's a healing angel who works beside Archangel Michael to replace negative energies with faith and compassion. Zadkiel helps us see the Divine light within ourselves and others, instead of focusing on the surface personality, behavioral mistakes, or the ego.

If you're having difficulty forgiving yourself or someone else, ask Zadkiel to intervene. He'll act like a chimney sweep who cleans your body, mind, and heart of unforgiveness. This doesn't mean that you're sanctioning someone's abusive behavior. It just means that you're no longer willing to cart around the emotional residue of old situations.

Archangel Zadkiel is also widely known for his help with memory functions. If you need to memorize important information, you need to remember where you put your car keys, or you just want to develop your memory in general, call upon Zadkiel.

Helps with:

- Compassion
- Finding lost objects
- Forgiveness of self and others
- Healing, emotionally and physically
- Memory enhancement
- Remembering important information
- Studies, students, and tests

INVOCATION

Anytime you feel upset, ask Zadkiel to intervene:

"Archangel Zadkiel, please help me heal my heart. If I'm holding on to unforgiveness, please help me release it fully. If there's something I'm not seeing, please help me to see clearly. If I need more compassion, please fill my heart with mercy. If I'm worried or anxious, please fill my heart with faith and calmness. I now surrender this situation fully to you and God, and I trust that your God-given healing power takes care of every detail with Divine grace, harmony, and wisdom. Thank you."

Artemis
(Greece)

Also known as *Artemis Calliste, Delia, Luna, Mother Artemis, Phoebe.*

Greek goddess of the new moon, with parallels to the Roman goddess Diana, Artemis is the daughter of Zeus and Leto. Her brother is Apollo.

Known as "the Huntress of Souls," Artemis carries a bow and arrow and spends most of her time in nature with the wood nymphs. She's a protectress of anyone who calls upon her, and particularly defends unmarried young women, children, and animals. However, she always protects nonviolently, using wisdom as her sole weapon. She's considered a nature, fertility, and moon goddess.

Artemis sets her sights on her goals, and as a result, she's a powerful manifestor. She teaches us the importance of spending time in nature, and to follow our intuition as we strive to become more natural and authentic humans.

I called upon Artemis just after the new moon.

"Power can be paralyzing," replied the pixielike woman with short-cropped hair, a beautiful large-eyed face, and ears slightly pointed on the top. She seemed to be captivated with hunting something, but I knew it wasn't an animal or a person. Artemis then told me that she was hunting metaphorical gold: *"I track down wisdom and experiences that I can later recount to children in the form of fairy tales. Today I'm mostly*

concerned with helping wisdom grow in upcoming generations. The children are unsure of their boundaries and limits. They know that they have power that can exceed that of their parents, so they hold back, unwilling to release this mighty power, for fear of overpowering their adult guardians.

"Children today feel unsafe unless their parents are more powerful than they are. That's why I work dually alongside parents of the young. I encourage them not to perpetuate a battle of wills with their offspring, but to assume their power for the sake of their children's own awareness and to balance and use their power with love."

Helps with:

- Animals and wildlife
- Camping and hiking
- Children, especially girls
- Environmentalism
- Fertility, child conception, and adoption
- Intuition, increasing and honoring
- Power, especially feminine
- Protection

INVOCATION

Go outside to call upon Artemis—preferably, stand barefoot on the earth, sand, soil, or grass. Then say:

"Artemis, I ask for your companionship and guidance in helping me open up my natural intuition and my feminine strength and power, which resides within each man and woman. I open my arms to your friendship and leadership. Help me reconnect with nature and my natural self. Help me honor my true feelings and stand up for what I know to be true, deep in my heart. Help me to be strong, wise, and beautiful in all ways. Thank you."

Ashtar
(New Age)

Also known as *Commander Ashtar.*

Ashtar is a human-looking mediator who works with extraterrestrials and humans, helping to create a peaceful Universe.

Ashtar is a member of the Great White Brotherhood [see the Glossary], and he works closely with Jesus, Archangel Michael, and Saint-Germain. Like a nightclub bouncer, Ashtar protects Earth from negative visitors or energies from other planets. He's involved with ensuring peace between planet populations through the Intergalactic Federation. He also heads a group of humans and extraterrestrials known as "the Ashtar Command."

Ashtar's mission is to avert nuclear war on Earth, which would have a negative ripple effect across many galaxies. He wants to help humans reach their highest potential (a process known as *ascension*) and be completely focused on Divine love. Ashtar guides humans away from third-dimensional thinking that believes in limits and restrictions and is focused on time measurement. He also gives personal guidance on how to stay safe and calm during the many changes occurring on Earth.

I attempted to contact Ashtar several times and was told that the best time to reach him was on a clear, starry evening, or while flying at high altitudes in an airplane. So I decided to combine the two and communicate with him while flying at 30,000 feet at night!

I've seen Ashtar and have been aware of his presence with many of my clients, especially those whom I call "Starpeople" (those who have a connection to other galaxies). He's the pale man with white hair portrayed on the "Support" card in my *Healing with the Angels* oracle deck and on the cover of my book about Starpeople, *Earth Angels*.

"I'm here," Ashtar said to me when our connection was complete. *"You felt me as warm love before you could hear me. I come from a different dimension, one that your conscious mind—while existing in third-dimensional, time-warped thinking—cannot as easily grasp as your soul can during its nightly sojourns to visit us for a higher education.*

"I won't encroach upon your missions, but I'm here if you need me. I promise to keep you safe from all outward invasions."

Helps with:

- Aliens, understanding and having peaceful interactions with
- Earth changes
- Profound thinking
- Protection
- Releasing fear
- Spiritual understanding

INVOCATION

Ashtar is easiest to connect with at night, when the stars are illuminated in the heavens. Hold your intention to contact him in your mind, and he'll come to you. If you have fears concerning aliens, Ashtar's presence with you will be subtle, as he's a loving being who doesn't want to evoke fear in any way.

Athena
(Greece)

Also known as *Pallas Athena, Athene.*

Athena's roots are ancient and multicultural; however, she's best known as the Greek warrior goddess of wisdom, household affairs, and arts and crafts.

Athena is the daughter of Zeus, and her temple was the Parthenon. Legends discuss Athena's courage and intuitive wisdom during battles. In artistic renderings, Athena is usually depicted with a breastplate, shield, and sword, and often accompanied by an owl. This bird has come to be associated with her, perhaps due to her wisdom.

When she bears the extra title "Pallas," Athena is known as a warrior goddess who protects, and who inspires women to exhibit their inner strength and have the courage to stand their ground. She encourages humans to use intuitive wisdom, rather than anger or violence, to heal arguments. In New Age teachings, Pallas Athena is regarded as an ascended master of the fifth ray of light, which is the ray concerning truthfulness and integrity.

When I called upon Athena, I saw a beautiful woman standing in a single-person chariot with metal wrist cuffs and a metallic headdress. Her energy was very intense, and she was panting, as if she'd just completed a sizable task.

"No job is too big for me," she said bluntly. *"I'm a taskmaster who gets*

the job before me done to full completion. Often I delegate to star beings."

Athena pointed out the stars in the sky, referring to them as sweet, living beings bearing the souls of innocent, loving children who are devoted to helping Athena. *"The whole universe breathes,"* she said in response to my unspoken questions about the stars. *"It reverberates with life, and there's no place where life is not—it is a continuous pattern of ever-moving energy that is everywhere, without exception. And that is how I handle my tasks at hand: by commanding the energy with the firm, loving touch of a determined parent. You can do the same."*

Helps with:

- Arguments, resolving
- Arts and artists
- Crafts and craftspeople
- Justice, attaining
- Protection, physical and psychical
- War, avoiding and resolving
- Writers and writing

INVOCATION

One way to invoke Athena is to say:

"Athena, I need your assistance, and request your powerful presence, please. Beloved sister, I ask for your intervention in my life. Please infuse every part of my existence with graceful strength: my thoughts, movements, relationships, and all situations with which I'm involved. I ask that you help my friends and family to accept and honor my new-found power. Please help me harness and use this strength in peaceful and loving ways. I thank you!"

Babaji
(Himalaya)

Also known as *Mahavatar Babaji, Shri Babaji.*

Made famous by Paramahansa Yogananda's book *Autobiography of a Yogi,* Babaji is known as "the deathless avatar" because he overcame physical limitations regarding the human life span. It's said that he didn't die, but ascended with his physical body. Many accounts of him appearing physically to spiritual seekers have been written. However, he usually comes to those who invoke him on the spiritual plane, and they "hear" Babaji through thoughts, feelings, or visions.

Babaji's mission is to bring humanity closer to God, and to follow God's will. He encourages people to follow their own spiritual path, and says that all religions lead to God. He encouraged Yogananda to bring Kriya Yoga (which involves 18 yoga postures—also known as *asanas* or *mudras*) to the West. Kriya is known as a tool of enlightenment and may have helped spark the current popularity in yoga.

Helps with:

- Addictions and cravings, overcoming or reducing
- Breathwork
- Clear communication with God

- Manifestation
- Materiality, detaching from
- Protection from religious persecution
- Simplifying your life
- Spiritual growth
- Yoga practice

INVOCATION

Say the name Babaji repeatedly, feeling the energy of his name in your heart. In his autobiography, Yogananda said that if you say Babaji's name with reverence, he directly blesses you. He told me that we can best contact him while we're engaged in breathwork and yoga. Babaji said that he's one with all breath, and when we consciously breathe in and out deeply, we're consciously connecting with him.

Brigit
(Ireland, Spain, France, and Wales)

Also known as *Brid, Brighid, St. Brigid, Brigantia,*
Mary of the Gaels, Bride, Brigid.

Brigit is a warrior goddess who has struck a perfect balance of femininity and no-apologies power. Depending upon whom you ask, her name either means "the bright one," "the bright arrow," or "the powerful one." All of these names describe Brigit perfectly.

Originally a highly respected Celtic goddess afforded much acclaim in ancient Ireland, Brigit had a shrine erected in her honor in the town of Kildare, where women tended to a flame that burned continually. In the fifth century, Brigit was adopted by the Catholic church and was deemed "Saint Brigid."

Brigit is the female equivalent of Archangel Michael, fiercely protecting and lovingly clearing those who call upon her. Like Michael, Brigit also inspires Divine guidance and prophetic information. She's the half-sister of the Celtic love god, Aengus, sharing the same mother with him. Brigit is known as a triple goddess of the flame who uses her flames to help purify us; and increase fertility, creativity, and promote healing. "Triple goddess" means that Brigit has three different personas or aspects, as if she's three different people, each with distinct duties and specialties.

Brigit is a sun goddess, associated with fire. When she's in your presence, you may feel hot and actually begin to perspire. Brigit is celebrated each February 1 during an event originally known as "Imbolc," the rite to usher in springtime and welcome the birth of new livestock.

I invoked Brigit while sitting by the Irish sea on a hot summer afternoon. Brigit appeared as a fiery redhead with beautiful, long, wavy hair. Her intensity surprised me at first, yet it was accompanied by loving confidence, like the sun that merely burns without any hint of anger, fear, or urgency. Brigit reminds me of a combination of Mother Mary, with her graceful feminine love, and Archangel Michael, with his no-nonsense commitment to purpose and protection. She's a "supermother," one who's simultaneously accessible and loving, yet fiercely protective without fail. I get the feeling that nothing can get past Brigit's impeccable protective power and energy.

She says: *"I'm the embodiment of fiery devotion to the good people of the planet Earth. At one time, I walked upon Earth, and my heart was broken in many ways by careless and thoughtless actions against myself, my people, and the land. The rest of my time I devoted to trying to understand human nature. I now have insight into the 'nature of the beast,' if you will, of the human heart. I see that its frailty lies in indecision and worry. Cast, therefore, your cares onto me, and I shall carry them away.*

"Humanity is heavy with grief now over the loss of innocence [**Author's note:** To me, this sentence seemed like a post-September 11 reference] *and the many rivalries that have been invented and imposed. These are artificial boundaries, and the committee with which I work seeks to blur the lines of these boundaries to build unity and salvation. Devotion to oneness at this time is essential, a single-pointed focus upon the One. Inside of each of us is a savior. Learn to invoke your internal savior as a counterbalance to cares and worries. Watch how this inner deity quietly and discreetly intervenes.*

"It's with these workings that we all come together—we who oversee the Mission on a grand scale, and all of those upon the planet who hold great desires to bring goodness home. This teamwork is built upon the framework and understanding of our oneness. It isn't difficult to understand the mechanics of these workings, as they're orchestrated for your higher good. I call it the workings of 'inner salvation'—instead of simply focusing upon

improving outward situations and other people's lives, try this instead: Go inward and explore the inner mission, the inner territory, the inner deities."

Helps with:

- Courage, increasing (especially for women)
- Life purpose and finding direction
- Protection
- Warmth—in relationships, body, and environment

INVOCATION

You can contact Brigit at any time; however, it's especially effective to light a candle and stare at its flame as you say:

> "Great Brigit, I know that you hear me the moment that I think of you. I ask for your presence and assistance. Please lend me your courage and power so that I may rise to the level of my highest capabilities. Please warm my heart and mind with your brightness, and burn away any thoughts, feelings, or behaviors that stand in the way of my Divine potential. Help me to have the courage to be my very best, and to lose all fear of being powerful."

Buddha
(Asia)

Also known as *Siddhartha Buddha, Buddha Goutama, Lord Goutama.*
The name Buddha means "the Enlightened or Awakened One."

Born on the full moon, May 8 (the exact year isn't agreed upon, but it's believed to be in the 500 B.C. era), Prince Goutama Siddhartha grew up wealthy behind palace walls, with every need taken care of. As he grew older and walked beyond the palace, he noticed poverty-stricken, diseased and elderly people, individuals that he had not previously been aware of. Determined to help alleviate the suffering that he witnessed, the prince renounced his royal title and wealth and left the palace.

However, Siddhartha's ascetic life didn't bring him the full enlightenment he desired. So he sat beneath a bodhi tree and vowed not to rise until he'd become fully enlightened. He breathed in and out deeply during the evening of a full moon, dispelling bodily cravings and fearful thoughts. Once he overcame these lower energies, he began recalling his past lives. This helped him see the endlessness of life, and he was filled with understanding as to how to overcome unhappiness, pain, and death. When he arose from sitting, he was a Buddha.

Buddha's teachings about detachment from suffering through inner peace became the basis for Buddhism. Because he had lived both extremes of living—as a rich prince and as an ascetic—Buddha proposed that the key to happy living was "the Middle Way," or moderation in all things.

You may find that Buddha is easier felt than heard. When you call upon him, you'll probably feel a swelling of warm love in your heart. That's his calling card, a sign that you've truly connected with his loving presence.

Helps with:

- Balance and moderation in all things
- Joy
- Peace, inner and world
- Spiritual growth and understanding

INVOCATION

Sit quietly, and focus upon the sound of your breath. Notice it slowing down as you listen. Feel and hear your heart beating in conjunction with your breath. Imagine that there's a magical door deep inside your being. It's a beautiful opening, decorated with powerful symbols and crystals.

From your heart, ask to connect with Buddha. Then imagine opening the door and seeing him there inside of you. Keep breathing deeply, feeling your connection through breath to beloved Buddha.

Fill your heart with his sweet kindness, his gentle power, and his surety. Feel the safety and peace that comes from being in his presence. Ask him any question that you like, feel the answer in your heart and body, and hear the answer whispered into your mind. Notice that all of Buddha's words are couched in utmost respect for you and everyone involved. Thank him after your meeting is concluded.

Cordelia
(England, Wales, Ireland)

Also known as *Creiddylad, Creudylad.*

Cordelia is the beautiful goddess of spring and summer flowers, and of flower fairies. Shakespeare portrayed Cordelia as the daughter of King Lear in his play of the same name. However, she's actually the daughter of the sea god, Lir, so she was born a sea goddess.

Cordelia is celebrated on May 1 during Beltane, an ancient celebration marking the beginning of summer, when the weather is warm enough to allow ranchers to let cattle out of their pens and into the fields.

Cordelia came to me while I sat on the grounds of Stonehenge, leaning against one of the ancient stones. She gave me this message: *"Merriment intertwined with ancient Celtic wisdom—I weave the stellar wisdom of astral energies with an infusion of pixie dust from the Earthly pollen of nature's wise ones. I'm an instrument of contradiction: the earth and the sky; the sunrise and the sunset; the cold and the heat. Extremes without compromise are a powerful combination. Feel them deep inside your ancient bones, connected with Mother Ground (what you call the Earth Mother). Your bones are borne of her, and in a continual loop will return to her once again.*

"Feel the freedom of releasing yourself from Earthly concerns and walking in the middle between Earth and her stars, unconcerned for anything

but joy, mirth, and playfulness as I help to teach you how to provide for all of your Earthly needs."

Helps with:

- Celebration
- Courage
- Gardening and flowers
- Joy
- Life changes
- Stress management

INVOCATION

Call upon Cordelia whenever you feel stressed or trapped indoors. You can "escape" from office routines by closing your eyes and imagining yourself standing in a field of flowers with her during a perfect springtime afternoon. Mentally say to her:

"Beautiful Cordelia, I come to you as a friend in need of some time off from duties and responsibilities. Please take my hand and bring me fresh air, freedom, and the fragrance of flowers. Carry me away for a much-needed respite. Renew my spirit and fill my heart with joy, laughter, and playfulness. Help me carry this high energy in my heart and mind for the rest of the day. Help me approach my responsibilities with joy. Thank you!"

Coventina
(United Kingdom)

Coventina is a Celtic goddess who oversees the sprites and water nymphs. She's a goddess of rain, rivers, lakes, streams, ponds, oceans, and water-based creatures. Coventina loves the cattails and lily pads by riverbanks. She heals those who swim in the water while invoking her. Coventina also helps with the growth of vegetation near beaches, rivers, lake fronts, and islands.

Because of her relationship to water, Coventina can swim into psychic domains and help with inspiration, psychic abilities, dreams, and prophecies. She's also associated with purification and cleanliness, and you can call upon her for a spiritual baptism to relieve you of worries and judgments, and to help you abstain from unhealthful and addictive substances.

In ancient times, people would throw coins into a well associated with Coventina to request her assistance. (This is believed to be the origin of the "wishing well.") Because of the bounty of coins, Coventina represents abundance in all ways. Legend also associates Coventina with flying fish, and today she can be invoked to fly in airplanes safely and fearlessly.

Since Coventina is primarily considered a British divinity (although she helps out worldwide), it was fitting that I talked with her while at the ancient stone circle temple, Stonehenge, in southern England. She told me, *"I will help anyone who is involved with ecological welfare, especially concerning water cleanliness, the preservation of water and its inhabitants, and water run-off issues. I'm dedicated to the whales, dolphins, and cetaceans."*

Helps with:

- Abundance
- Dolphins and cetaceans
- Environmentalism
- Healing with water
- Psychic abilities and prophecy
- Purification and cleanliness
- Swimming
- Water cleanliness and supply

INVOCATION

Coventina works with us in our dreams, if we call to her before going to sleep. She'll bring the higher selves of dolphins and whales alongside her. Together, they will give you high-level messages that you may not remember the next morning, but whose information will be incorporated into your subconscious mind, where it will help you with answers and guidance. So, before going to sleep, say to her:

"Coventina, I ask that you and your dolphin and whale companions enter my dreams tonight and take me above the third-dimensional plane to the place of answers and wisdom. [Ask her any questions that you would like answered during the night.] Thank you for your help and strong support."

Damara
(United Kingdom)

Damara's name means "gentle." She's a sweet and docile goddess of home and hearth who helps with family harmony—that is, maintaining peaceful energy within the domestic realm. Damara also assists with the manifestation of money to help pay for family expenses.

She says, *"I'm happy to heal, guide, and help you feel the heat of love, passion, and deep caring unadulterated by fear or worry. I'm also glad to help heal children's cuts, bruises, and hurt feelings. I'm especially available to help families with young children. I will gladly guide a mother in decision-making for her family's welfare. And if the woman is considering decisions about whether to divorce or leave her children's father, she can call upon me for input and assistance."*

Helps with:

- Abundance—especially for household needs
- Children, guiding and healing
- Home, peace within the
- Manifestation—especially for family and household needs

Invocation

Call upon Damara whenever you need help with household relationships, including those with your spouse, live-in partner, roommate, parents, or children—in other words, if you need intervention with anyone with whom you're living. Here's an example of how to contact her. Close your eyes and think:

"Damara, I need your help right away, please! I ask that you go to [name of person in household you need help with] and discuss my desire for peace and harmony. Please let [name] know that I'm a loving person with good intentions. Please help [name] to drop all judgments about me, and for me to do the same, in turn. Damara, I ask that you fill our home with so much energy of love that nothing else can exist. When anyone enters this home, they're healed. I'm so grateful for this intervention, Damara."

Dana
(Ireland)

Also known as *Danu, Danann.*

Dana's name is rooted in the Old Irish word *Dan,* which means "knowledge." She is a powerful Celtic creator goddess, believed to be a Great Mother aspect of the Divine Creator. Historians say that she has the most ancient roots of any Celtic deity, esteemed by the pre-Gaelic Tuatha Dé Danaans, a group of alchemists in Ireland. When the Gaelics overtook Ireland, legend says that the Tuatha Dé Danaans became the leprechauns who today inhabit Ireland.

When I invoked Dana while sitting on a bluff overlooking the Irish sea, I first saw a coat similar to one that a king might sport—regal and bejeweled. Next, I saw a king's crown. "But Dana is a female deity!" I mentally protested. Then I saw her—not as I expected her to look (my mental image was that she'd look like someone's eccentric aunt). Instead, I saw a rational, young-looking woman who emanated wisdom and intelligence.

Dana placed the crown on my head and the coat over my shoulders. I started to argue, but she stopped me. *"You're all royalty,"* Dana explained, meaning all of humanity, *"and you need to allow me the honor of dignifying you all with my services."*

I could tell that Dana didn't mean that she'd perform every feat of manifestation for us, but she assured me that her energy was *"magically intertwined with each act of magical manifestation."* She said, *"Remember that I'm just another aspect of God, and that your Western master teacher Jesus taught you that you are all gods."*

Dana showed me wavelengths of energy, all intertwined like parallel lines of rope, and said that each of us was part of those wavelengths. Her wavelength was often the foundation, bottom, or supporting line of energy that we could rest upon. *"Let nature do its course as you perform miracles,"* she added. And again she emphasized that we're all kings, queens, gods, and goddesses . . . deities in our own right: *"You're deities in the making, as you test out your own skills with chaperones like me by your side."*

Helps with:

- Abundance
- Alchemy and Divine magic
- Animals, healing
- Children, fertility, and mothering
- Elemental kingdom, meeting and working with the (particularly leprechauns)
- Worthiness, self-esteem, and deservingness issues

INVOCATION

Wear, look at, or hold something that makes you feel abundant—or even better—that makes you feel like royalty. This could mean going to a jewelry store and trying on a beautiful ring, or looking at a photograph of an opulent estate. Imagine yourself with unlimited resources, and feel a sense of total financial security. Even if you can imagine and experience this sensation for just a brief time, that's enough. Then mentally say to Dana:

"Dana, thank you for lending me your magical abilities, which I now use in the service of joy, fun, and support of my Divine mission. Thank you for your generosity in showing me how to accept these resources, and how to enjoy them. Thank you for helping me receive without guilt, and to know that I deserve this attention and support and that it will ultimately allow me to help the planet."

Devi
(India)

Also known as *Ambika, Ghagavati, Devee, Ida, Shakti.*

Devi is a Hindu or Vedic goddess who is known as the "Universal" or "Great" mother. The "Mother" in the term *Mother-Father God,* she's the female energy of God. Devi, therefore, is the embodiment of God-power: absolute, creative, and supportive. She's one of India's most important and powerful goddesses.

The term *Devi* is sometimes used generically to describe any goddess. All goddesses are considered to be aspects of the One Devi, who is the female energy of the One Creator.

As I called upon Devi while sitting on a bluff overlooking the Pacific off the Kona coast in Hawaii, I first felt a motherly energy feed me a sweet-tasting substance. It felt like Mom was giving me a treat.

Devi said, *"Let me sweeten your palate* [similar to cleansing your palate] *so that you can fully taste, hear, and understand my joyful message. Cleansing is a vital first step, allowing even greater messages of love to come through.*

"Drop all thoughts of worldly possessions as you hear my call. The world needs you to minister to the grief that permeates the very essence of others' souls. I'm pushing you toward compassion in action—taking steps to heal the world's aching grief.

"My heart swells with love and gratitude for those who reach out in service and kindness for people in need. You cannot be devastated by loss when your heart is fixed upon helping others. It takes you out of self-consciousness

71

when you're attuned to ministering to others.

"I'm here to minister alongside you so that you can feed the populace's hungry hearts and bodies. I want to protect young children from growing wary of love and becoming frozen in their hearts. Hell is literally when people's hearts freeze over, rendering them cold and useless and preventing them from participating in the planet's heart song.

"Many individuals are growing restless at this juncture, and they need shepherding into the new atmosphere that embraces love and love's manifestations."

Helps with:

- Addictions, releasing and detoxification from
- Meaningfulness—finding more in life and career
- Purification of body and mind
- Relationships, all aspects of

INVOCATION

Devi is best contacted while sitting alone in nature, either in a comfortable chair or on the sand, grass, or ground. Wrap your arms around yourself in an embrace, and imagine that Devi is joining you, giving you a hug. Feel her love in your heart and body, and breathe it in even deeper with a long inhalation and slow exhalation. Mentally ask her to come into your heart, mind, and body and purify away any toxins, staleness, darkness, or hardening of your feelings. Feel her beams of loving energy directed throughout your body, and know that she's carefully purifying you in the most thorough yet gentle way. You may find that you twitch as she releases lower energies. When your body feels still, stay in mental communion with her as long as you feel comfortable. Ask her to help you stand up, and feel the renewal of energy in your body. Give thanks to Devi, and make plans to be with her often.

Diana
(Rome)

Also known as *Diana of Ephesus*.

Sharing attributes similar to that of the Greek goddess Artemis, Diana is a moon goddess who helps with fertility and abundance.

The daughter of the chief god, Jupiter, Diana is called the goddess of childbirth because her mother bore her painlessly. Immediately after Diana was born, she helped with the birth of her twin brother, Apollo.

Diana is associated with bathing and purification. At the Temple of Diana in Ephesus, Turkey (one of the largest temples in the ancient world, and one that is noted in Acts 19 in the Bible), female followers would engage in ritual hair-washing at Diana's shrine.

Diana spends time with elementals, and forest and wood nymphs. She is particularly fond of women, and also helps lesbians with relationship and societal issues. She's usually depicted with the bow and arrow that her father gave to her as a young girl, symbolizing female strength and power.

One night as the moon was waxing, Diana said to me, *"I help you* [meaning everyone] *rise above all Earthly concerns, in the same way that the moon hovers above the earth. Be like the moon, shining light gaily upon others, and then like the new moon, regularly withdrawing for personal respite.*

"The moon isn't afraid to shine, nor does it fear attention, ridicule, or rejection. These lower fears sink Earthlings into despair and depression because the soul knows that it's capable of so much more! The soul doesn't like

to be harnessed or restrained—oh, no! Unleash yourself completely, so that I may shine upon you as a reflection of your outwardly manifested holiness."

Helps with:

- Animals—breeding, pregnancy, and birthing
- Childbirth, painless
- Elementals, connecting with
- Lesbian concerns
- Twins

INVOCATION

Diana's connection is especially strong on moonlit nights. However, you can always contact her at any time.

"Diana, please help me shine brightly like you. Assist me in releasing anxieties about ridicule or rejection so that I may enjoy being my true self fully. Take me to a higher place, where I may best serve humanity as a shining example of one who listens to inner wisdom, love, and guidance. Help my life to be full, very full, of light. Thank you."

El Morya
(Theosophical Society; New Age)

El Morya is a new ascended master, first recorded in the 1880s by Madame Blavatsky, founder of the Theosophical Society, and repopularized in the 1960s by Mark and Elizabeth Clare Prophet and other authors of the "I AM Teachings."

El Morya appears to be based upon an actual man named Ranbir Singh, son of Raja Gulab Singh, who was the ruler of Kashmir in the 1840s. Kashmir was threatened with takeover by the British in 1845, but Raja Singh paid a ransom to convince the British to leave the country alone. When the Raja died in 1858, Ranbir became Maharaj of Kashmir.

Historians hail Ranbir for unifying the states of Nagar and Hunza, and for creating humane and fair civil and criminal laws. Ranbir was quite popular among his constituents. He passed away in 1885, the same time that Madame Blavatsky was writing her channeled books about the ascended masters. Blavatsky claimed to have spent time with El Morya in India, and she may have been protecting a friendship with Ranbir by giving him a pseudonym.

Blavatsky's Theosophical Society defines the term *Morya* as "the name of a Rajpoot tribe, so-called because of its being almost altogether composed of the descendants of the famous Moryan sovereign of Marya-Nagara. The Moryan Dynasty began with certain Kshatriyas of the Sakya line closely related to Goutama Buddha, who founded the town of

Morya-Nagara in the Himalayas." Blavatsky, and later, Elizabeth Clare Prophet, did make reference to El Morya being a "Rajput prince" and a "Tibetan Mahatma," both apt descriptions of Ranbir.

When I invoked El Morya, he came to me rapidly in a most extraordinary way. The man that I saw closely matched the paintings that Blavatsky had made of El Morya, although I purposely didn't look at her artwork until after my channeling of El Morya.

"Put aside your cares, concerns, and worries, and come to me," I was told. A brown-skinned man, slightly heavyset with a glowing smile of love and arms outstretched, faced me. *"Let me embrace you and perform an energy transfusion, replacing faithlessness with faith."* I melted into his young-grandpa-like embrace, felt my breath become deeper, and experienced a tingling sensation throughout my hands, wrists, calves, and feet.

El Morya explained that he was surmounting my inner obstacles, which he said were walls of defenses that I'd built up as misguided shields. *"So much better to use these instead,"* he said, holding up two beautifully ornate shields. *"This is a heart protector, and this one is for the small of your back—two vulnerable areas for lightbearers like you. Through a form of psychic surgery, I shall permanently install these shields deep into the chasm of your being, protecting you from harm of any sort.*

"These shields will allow problems to roll off of you like butter on a heated surface." He explained that these shields were a buffer to tone down impulsiveness based on emotionally based decisions not tempered by wisdom.

"I'm so glad that you called upon me, and I invite all who read these words to do the same. I shall install shields at their request, individually attuned to each person's energy field. The shields can always be removed at the blink of an eye, should you say the word. However, I'm certain that you'll feel much better and more grounded as a result, and will be comforted by their placement."

Helps with:

- Decision-making
- Faith
- Groundedness
- Protection—especially energy and psychic

INVOCATION

"Beloved El Morya, who serves the Divine light, please come to me now. Escort me to the place of selfless service where Divine assignments are made. Shield me from the negative thoughts of my own mind, as well as negative energy in general. Help me stay centered in my commitment to learn, grow, heal, and teach with a positive intent and positive energy. Thank you."

Forseti
(Norse)

Also known as *Forete*.

The Norse god of justice, fairness, arbitration, and reconciliation, Forseti, whose name means "presiding one," stills all strife; in other words, he's the ultimate peacemaker. He's an arbitrator in Heaven, listening to both points of view in arguments, and creating win-win solutions. He resolves differences with love so that everyone involved in the original dispute is persuaded to reconcile.

I spoke with him at twilight atop the monolithic stones of the Joshua Tree National Park in California, where he said, *"I'm here, guiding your trail at every turn. The wheels of justice seem to move slowly, but I'm behind the scenes, working tirelessly on your behalf. Whatever legal ties or angles seem to be thrown at you, I'm here to bounce them straightaway. Think of me as the ultimate lawyer of legal peace and justice—I'm free of cost, I make house calls, and I respond to your entreaties immediately."*

Helps with:

- Arguments, resolving
- Fairness
- Legal matters, resolving

- Peace
- Protection—especially legal in nature
- Truth issues

INVOCATION

Call upon Forseti when legal matters arise, or are threatened. He goes to work on your behalf immediately:

"Dear Forseti, I ask for your intervention into this situation, to promote an awareness of kindness and fairness. Thank you for the peaceful resolution of this dispute, which is now being completely resolved."

Ganesh
(Hindu; India)

Also known as *Ganesha*.

Ganesh is an elephant-headed deity who removes obstacles for anyone who asks for his help. He is the Hindu god of prosperity and wisdom, who also assists with writing and art projects. Many different stories abound that explain why Ganesh has an elephant's head. In most stories, Ganesh lost his head (perhaps because of his father's anger), and Ganesh's mother took the first head that she could find—a baby elephant's—and placed it on her son's neck.

In Hinduism, Ganesh is the first deity contacted during prayers. It's recommended that you invoke Ganesh prior to conducting a ceremony, engaging in writing, or before any endeavor in which you want to succeed.

Ganesh is extremely loving, sweet, polite, and gentle, yet also very strong. He's large enough to blaze trails ahead of you so that your path is clear, but he's also so filled with love and sweetness that you don't have to worry that his brute strength could turn against you. He's analogous to Archangel Michael, in that he's a loving and loyal protective force.

Ganesh is called "the Remover of Obstacles" because he mows down any blocks that could stand in his path. Think of a tame elephant walking ahead of you on a trail, trampling brush so that your way is clear. That is Ganesh.

I was having difficulty at airports at one time because security guards kept stopping me to open and search my carry-on bags. Since my husband and I travel nearly every weekend, I quickly grew weary of these frequent suitcase searches. I wanted the security personnel to ignore me and just let me through without stopping me. So, I placed a small statue of Ganesh in my carry-on bag. From that moment on, my bags were never again searched.

Ganesh immediately comes to those who call upon him. For example, I was on the telephone talking with my friend Johnna following the death of her mother. I was consoling her when I suddenly saw a clairvoyant image of Ganesh next to her. I said, "Johnna, did you call on Ganesh?" And she answered, "Yes! I'm wearing a necklace with a medallion of Ganesh on it. I've been rubbing the picture all day, calling for Ganesh to be with me."

Ganesh says, *"I see all obstacles as being surmountable; in fact, I don't see obstacles at all, and that's the point: All barriers in your path are self-imposed. They represent your decision to be afraid of moving forward. You cast your fear outward by projecting thoughts into the future, worried that either this or that may occur. Your worries about the future have created blocks and boogeymen that you will meet on your future path. But don't worry—since they're your own creation, you can will them away.*

"Ask me to assist, and I puncture the balloons of dark illusions. Even if you've managed to manifest a worst-case scenario, call upon me to heal and guide you. All thought-forms are on a level playing field, and no matter how dire the appearance, they're all equally surmountable. I plow through them all quite easily with my unwavering faith in 'all good, all love.' That's the only power that exists. The rest are all unreal illusions. Let them go and know the truth of all situations: God and love always prevail."

Helps with:

- Abundance
- Artistic projects
- Household peace and harmony
- Obstacles, removing and avoiding

- Wisdom issues
- Writing

INVOCATION

If you're unfamiliar with how Ganesh looks, find a picture of him in a book or on the Internet. Once you're familiar with his visage, it's easy to call upon him by visualizing him in your mind and saying:

> "Beloved Ganesh, thank you for smoothing my path today, with harmony and peacefulness reigning supreme. I appreciate your walking before me, clearing all obstructions that could impede my progress. Help me see the blessings within everything today. Thank you."

Guinevere
(United Kingdom)

Also known as *Gwenhwyfar*.

Guinevere, whose name means "white one," is a goddess of love relationships, fertility, and motherhood—and she also works with the
flower fairies. Her painting graces the cover of this book.

She's the Celtic triple goddess behind the story of King Arthur,
Camelot, and the Round Table. At Glastonbury Abbey in southern
England, two graves are marked with placards indicating that King
Arthur and Guinevere may be buried there. The Abbey is magical,
sacred, and filled with white doves—one of my favorite places on Earth.
It's not hard to imagine that Arthur and Guinevere would rest in such
an enchanting place.

I invoked Guinevere at Avebury, which is an ancient magical stone
circle (similar to Stonehenge, but much larger) in southern England. I
asked her, "What do you most want to help us with?"

Guinevere replied, *"Romantic entanglement is my specialty, for I have
empathetic resonance with every woman who has suffered the fate of feeling
unloved or unlovable in quest of romance. Any woman who feels she's on the
wrong foot 'in a man's world'—walking on uncharted territory—should
explore this world with me as her steady companion."*

Helps with:

- Romantic love, enhancing and finding
- Women's issues

INVOCATION

Draw a heart and stare at it while you call on Guinevere for help with romantic concerns:

> "Sister Guinevere, you appreciate the depth of love within my heart, and my capacity to give to another. You understand my desires completely. I now give you permission to intervene as my romantic intermediary, preparing me for a wonderful relationship, and opening my heart and mind to profound love infused with spirituality, honor, trust, and commitment. Thank you for helping me be with my One True Love without delay."

Then kiss the drawing of the heart, and hold it to your chest. Imagine that it's your Beloved Soulmate, and send loving energy to this person (even if you're not yet aware of who it might be). Ask Guinevere to help you maintain faith in romantic love.

Hathor
(Egypt)

Also known as *Athor, Athyr, Hat-hor, Hat-Mehit, Hawthor, Tanetu, The Celestial Cow, Queen of the Earth, Mother of Light, The Eye of Ra.*

Hathor is the ancient and beloved Egyptian goddess of the sun, sky, newborns, and the dead. Her celebrations were marked with a lot of drinking, music, and dancing, so Hathor is considered to be a patron of music, dance, and mirth. She's also associated with feminine beauty, cosmetics, fashionable clothing, and romantic relationships.

Hathor is a love and fertility goddess who helps bring soulmates together, oversees conception, protects pregnant mothers, acts as a midwife, and helps with raising children. As a multipurpose goddess responsible for nurturing all newborns, as well as helping the dead cross peacefully to the underworld, Hathor divided herself into seven goddesses to get everything done. She was then referred to as "the Hathors."

She says, *"When it comes to fairness, the heart already knows what the truth is. So, I do not judge—I simply lead the person inward quietly so that they can hear the decision of their heart.*

"I'm not here to chase down or interrogate anyone—that's not my role at all. I'm more like a guide along the most vital trek of all, that which entails making decisions regarding 'How shall I live my life?' Each and every moment affords us ample opportunities to seek and grow. Rest is a part of the operation, too, to be sure.

"But indecision leads us away from ourselves, and ultimately, then, from our Creator-Source. Indecision rests upon the inability to hear and trust the voice of one's own heart. My role, then, is to send my magical energy outward to those who request my assistance through prayer, worry, or even casual conversation.

"Those who are prepared, absorb my rays, which tip the scales of indecision in the direction of the true heart's desires. In this way, I'm a truth detector; however, it's up to each individual to summon courage to see and live their own truth."

Helps with:

- Artistic projects
- Beauty, attractiveness, and cosmetics
- Celebrations, music, parties, and dancing
- Children, conceiving, pregnancy, and parenting
- Decision-making
- Soulmate, finding one's

INVOCATION

Hathor loves dance and music, so play music and sway or dance as you contact her:

"Dear Hathor, I now surrender my decision to you, my higher self, and the Creator, and I get out of the way. Thank you for helping me make the best possible decision for the highest good for everyone concerned. Please help me clearly hear the decision within my mind and heart, and give me the courage and energy to follow that guidance."

Horus
(Egypt, Greece)

Also known as *Har, Harendotes, Harmakhet, Haroeris, Har-pa-Neb-Taui, Harseisis, Harpokrates, Hor, Horos, Ra-Harakhte.*

Horus is a powerful falcon-headed sky and sun god representing strength and victory. His father, Osiris, was killed by his uncle, Seth. His mother, Isis, magically brought Osiris back to life just long enough to conceive Horus. Then Seth killed Osiris again and dismembered his body so that he couldn't be revived. To avoid Seth's murderous actions, Isis bore and raised Horus in the papyrus marshes of Buto. Isis used the magical skills she'd learned from Ra and Thoth to keep Horus safe.

When Horus was a young man, he fought Seth to avenge his father's death. During the battle, one of Horus's eyes was injured. Eventually, Horus won the throne of both upper and lower Egypt. After that, Horus represented strength, victory, and justice. Every pharaoh in ancient Egypt was considered a living incarnation of Horus.

Horus appears as a falcon head with a large eye (the uninjured one) representing the third eye of clairvoyance. This all-seeing eye also helps us see the truth in all situations.

My experience with Horus (who has been one of my guides for some time) is that he doesn't talk much, but is more of a man of action. He puts his falcon eye up to your third eye, like a lens that gives you clearer psychic vision and insights into any situation on your mind. He helps you see the current truth about issues and how to heal the situation.

Horus's magical healing formula is: to see all people in the situation through the eyes of love. See them as being sweet, loving, and pure . . . which they are in spiritual truth.

Helps with:

- Clairvoyance
- Courage
- Mother-son relationships
- Standing your ground
- Strength
- Vision, physical and psychic

INVOCATION

You can call upon Horus to help you with spiritual or physical vision. The invocation can be done with your eyes either open or shut. You'll probably feel a tingling in your head, especially around the eyes and between the eyebrows when you say this invocation:

"Dear Horus, please lend me your eye so that I may see clearly. I ask for your intervention into my vision in all ways. Open my third eye fully so that I may see spiritually like you! Open my physical vision so that I may see clearly like you! Open my mind's eye completely so that I may see the inner plane like you! Thank you for clear sight. Thank you for releasing me from fear completely. Thank you for opening my eyes fully, that I may drink in the delicious sight of truth and beauty."

Ida-Ten
(Japan)

Also known as *Idaten.*

Ida-Ten is the Japanese god of law, truth, purity, legal victory, and justice.

A protector of monasteries, he has miraculous speed. As a mortal, he was a handsome young general in charge of protecting Buddhist monks, and Buddhism itself. Ida-Ten can guard against religious persecution or help you avert ridicule with respect to your spiritual beliefs.

As quiet as a church mouse, this mild-mannered deity whispers powerful, provocative advice into your ear regarding legal moves and maneuvers. Highly ethical, Ida-Ten nonetheless says, *"I consider lawsuits a form of sport wherein the champion exhibits superior wit, outsmarting the other like in a game of chess."*

Helps with:

- Justice
- Lawsuits, winning
- Protection against religious or spiritual persecution
- Protection of spiritual centers
- Truth issues

INVOCATION

Ida-Ten can be contacted as you're coming out of meditation to seal your practice with positive energy. Mentally say to him:

> "Precious Ida-Ten, all-loving and protective force from above, please surround my spiritual project now. Insulate me from all forms of fear so that I may be spared any harsh treatment or words. Prevent me from making judgments of any kind, and help me walk in truth while avoiding controversy. Peace is my true desire, Ida-Ten. Thank you."

Ishtar

(Assyria, Babylonia, Mesopotamia)

Also known as *Absus, Inanna.*

A Babylonian mother and warrior goddess with multiple unique traits ranging from gentleness to motherly protection, Ishtar is also invoked for healing physical pain and maladies.

She's associated with Venus, and some even believe her to be the embodiment of the planet itself. Ishtar openly displays her sensuality, and this may be why some fundamentalists have judged and rejected her.

As I invoked Ishtar, I clairvoyantly saw a picture of me standing with lots of ants crawling near my feet. Ishtar showed me that lower energies or thought-forms were similar to a herd of ants and other insects crawling on the ground—distracting and irritating if they crawled on one's feet, but ultimately not dangerous.

She then shined a beam of light from above my head, downward, which formed a circle around me, as if I were standing in a shower of bright light. The ants couldn't penetrate the light, nor did they want to. They would crawl right up to the light and then bounce back as if they'd just run into a wall of glass.

Ishtar said, *"Allow me the pleasure and honor of draping you in this robe of light, darling. I'm at your service, and know that this doesn't diminish my ability to perform humble service. I know that the noblest of professions is to shine beams of light to cast away shadows and to illuminate the highest of Divine wisdom. Make no mistake about it: I'm here to ease and eliminate pain, suffering, and sorrow through my protective stance.*

"Allow me to shield you with my barriers of light that only allow love to come shining through, and filter out negativity in all forms. A positive new day shines for you, as you are draped in my robe of loving light. Drink it in, Dear One. Quench your thirsty soul away from all fear."

Helps with:

- Child conception and parenting
- Compassion
- Healing, all kinds of
- Gentleness
- Love relationships and marriage
- Protection against lower energies
- Sexuality
- War, prevention or resolution of
- Weather

INVOCATION

Burn a white candle and stare at the flame, or stare at any light source as you speak to Ishtar. This is an especially effective invocation if you've just experienced a negative situation and wish to shake off its effects:

"Divine Ishtar, I stand in the midst of pure light with you now. Thank you for draping me in this light and showering me with the energy of love. I thirst for this love, so please quench me now. Wash away all effects of fear, and unleash me from others' fearful thoughts completely. Release me, release me, release me. Intervene with the others involved in this situation and rinse away any remaining ill feelings. I'm now free, and everyone involved is free as well. This is the truth. Thank you, Ishtar."

Isis
(Egypt)

Also known as Divine Mother, Goddess of the Mysteries, Goddess of Nature, Isis Myrionymos, Lady of Magic, Lady of Sacred Sexuality, Mistress of Hermetic Wisdom.

Isis is a multifunctional Egyptian moon goddess who embodies femininity, motherhood, magic, healing, and power. She married her brother Osiris and launched on a career teaching women across Egypt about home-life skills. While she was away, her other brother Seth murdered Osiris. Upon discovering the murder, Isis helped revive her husband from the dead, and they conceived a son, Horus.

Egyptian scholars regard Isis as the original high-priestess of magic. Legend says that Isis convinced Ra to reveal his secret name to her. Once she heard the name, Isis was automatically privileged to receive a complete understanding of high magic. (Thoth, the god of high magic, helped her refine and direct her knowledge.) It's said that Isis used a magical rod for her healings and manifestations, and used rattles to remove negative energies and lower spirits.

Isis is considered an Underworld Queen due to her resuscitation of her dying (and then dead) husband, and also due to her work escorting the dead in general. Her protective wings are engraved around Egyptian sarcophaguses, as they symbolize Isis's ability to renew the souls of the dead.

When I called upon Isis, I heard her say, *"I am Isis, Egyptian queen of the Nile!"* And there she was: a beautiful woman wearing a shawl of large bird wings outstretched like the largest eagle's wing span. She was very feminine, thin, and elegant—the epitome of classiness. She was constantly observing, watching everything like a hawk. I could tell that she had a blunt, to-the-point side to her, expressing her powerful leadership qualities.

She said, *"Have patience with yourself* [she meant everyone, in a universal sense] *while you're still growing and learning. Give countless thanks to yourself for your baby steps along the way. Although they may seem insignificant to you, they're major milestones for your inward self.*

"Celebrate each step," Isis repeated. *"As you appreciate every task that you complete, every kindness that you exhibit, everything—no matter how seemingly small—very soon life takes on the quality of a grand celebration. This is the antithesis of separation from the Divine, and it's your magic elixir for the ages."*

A beautiful friend of mine, Insiah Beckman, had a powerful experience with Isis when she traveled to Egypt in 1999. She's been actively working with Isis ever since. She told me:

"In Egypt, I became one with all life near the Temple of Isis. I could hear the ground, the pebbles, the grass, the Nile, the trees, and everything around me speak. I heard these beautiful voices say to me: 'Welcome home! Welcome home! You have come home again. This is where you lived many, many lifetimes ago!'

"A message was then channeled to me to reclaim who I am and begin my work. I knew then that I incorporated the energy of the goddess Isis that I had left behind in my last lifetime on Earth. The Isis energy is the energy of the Divine Mother— it's the loving and nurturing energy that all the Divine Mothers carry. I believe that they are one and the same, and that they're reincarnations in different forms and cultures to meet the times.

"My experience is this expansiveness that I feel at times, when my heart and energy field totally open up and incorporate all life with love and compassion. My prayer every day is for love, peace, understanding, and respect among all cultures, races, religions, and all life. I abhor any form of disharmony that puts my energy field totally out of sync."

Helps with:

- Divine magic
- Feminine strength, power, and beauty
- Joy
- Self-esteem

INVOCATION

Picture Isis standing behind you with her eagle wings extended, as if you have wings yourself. As you breathe, feel her power infused within you. Notice the loving and graceful energy of her strength. Be aware of the blissful feelings of peace as you say:

"Beautiful Isis, goddess of peaceful power, please infuse me with your graceful strength and your loving confidence. Help me be like you: refined, poised, confident, and loving. Help me soar like an eagle in all ways, inspiring and helping others as I fly high. Thank you."

Isolt
(Celtic)

Also known as *Esyllt, Iseult, Isolde, Ysolt, Ysonde.*

Isolt is the goddess of love and passion in relationships, who helps enhance sexual satisfaction, and offers assistance in finding a soulmate. Princess Isolt was the daughter of an Irish king during the reign of Arthur of Camelot. The various and conflicting legends about her passionate and tragic romantic entanglements with Tristan, prince of Cornwall, have earmarked Isolt as a goddess to the lovelorn.

I invoked her while sitting in an inverted boat that had been made into a temple, high above the Irish sea on a misty morning. Before any spirits would agree to talk with me on this day, the fairies first asked me to remove trash that someone had left on the sand. Once I did so, they opened the way for my transmissions.

I then called upon Isolt, the goddess of passion and sex. I was told that she was out of range "at a very high frequency." Finally, as I invoked further, I was clairvoyantly shown a rainbow with lightning bolts radiating from its underside. *"Isolt is a ray,"* I was told, a heavenly energy of deep, genuine, playful, and all-consuming love. *"Sprinkle it on any occasion like sugar,"* I was told playfully. Far more than a heroic goddess entity, Isolt is an energy beam that spreads when we tap in to it. I was told that we can use it for our love lives whenever and as often as possible. It's healing, and also aphrodisiac-like in its attracting power.

Helps with:

- Breakups, separations, and divorces—healing from
- Passion, reigniting
- Romantic love, attracting

INVOCATION

Put your hand on your chest and feel your heart beating. Imagine rainbow-colored rays of energy emanating from your hand, encircling your heart. Then call on Isolt:

"Loving Isolt, please send passionate energy filled with healthy and romantic love through my hand and into my heart. Thank you for healing anything that could block me from enjoying passion and romance completely. Thank you for opening my heart to true love."

Jesus
(Judeo-Christian)

Also known as *Jeshua, Lord and Savior, Lord Jesus, Christ, Sananda.*

What we know about Jesus of Nazareth comes from the four Gospels and the letters of Paul in the New Testament. Since the Gospels were written 70 or more years after the physical passing of Jesus, it's obvious that none of the authors met Jesus during his human lifetime. Their accounts, then, are based upon secondhand (or more) information passed down through time. No historian who lived during the time of Jesus' human life mentioned him in written accounts of that time period. Yet, there's no arguing the impact that this man has made on humanity up to the present day. Everything from the Gregorian calendar to religious institutions, from wars to spiritual healings, are based on his life in some way.

Many people report seeing apparitions of Jesus, and they often experience miraculous healings as a result. My books *Angel Visions* and *Angel Visions II* contain several stories about Jesus' miraculous powers. Testimony also comes from those who pray for Jesus' intervention . . . who then witness a miracle that they *know* was a result of those prayers. Other people report feeling deep love and comfort when they sense Jesus' presence near, or within, them.

Many have studied Jesus' approach to healing sickness, and they've applied those principles to garner impressive results. Many Christian and New Thought churches emphasize Jesus' teachings about love and forgiveness, and promote these methods as ways to cure personal and worldly ills.

There's a widespread belief that Jesus is watching over the world and its inhabitants, ensuring that harm doesn't befall us. In New Age circles, Jesus is believed to be the head of the Great White Brotherhood, a committee of great spiritual teachers and healers overseeing the spiritual renaissance on the planet.

My own experiences with Jesus are lifelong and extensive. I call upon him before every healing session, and have always found him to be the greatest healer among my friends in the spirit world. He is equally powerful with people and divinities of all religious and nonreligious backgrounds, and emanates unconditional love that can heal someone plagued by guilt, fear, and unforgiveness.

Helps with:

- Clear communication with God
- Divine guidance and direction
- Faith issues
- Forgiveness
- Healing of all kinds
- Manifestation
- Miracles

INVOCATION

Picture Jesus standing in front of you. From your heart, send him as much love as you can feel and imagine. Notice what happens next: The love is returned to you, magnified manyfold. Keep sending and receiving this love, monitoring your breath to make sure that you're breathing in this healing energy.

At the same time, mentally tell Jesus anything that's bothering you, minor or major. Pour your heart out to him, and reveal your deepest secrets—he's absolutely trustworthy and will always use this information in a positive way. Then, ask him to intervene and give you direction as to how to heal the situation. Don't tell him *how* to heal it; just know that it's in his loving hands, and that he will work directly with God to create a peaceful resolution for everyone involved. Give thanks in your heart, and let go.

Kali
(Hindu; India)

Also known as *Black Mother, Kali-Ma, Raksha-Kali.*

Kali is a Hindu aspect of Devi, who is the ultimate goddess. Kali is the goddess of the endings of cycles, the death and transformation energy that lets go of the old and brings in the new. Some are threatened by Kali's seemingly destructive power; however, Kali is actually a loving energy that helps free us of fear. She only destroys that which could keep us in bondage, or which could slow or divert our Divine mission, in the same way that a loving mother would take away dangerous items from her children.

Kali has the personality of a high-energy, supercharged woman on a clear mission. She has an impatient artist's temperament, like a stage mom who knows what needs to be done and doesn't have time to argue. She says, *"My passions have overwhelmed many who have likened me to a silver storm of fury. They've called me fickle, temperamental, and wrathful. Yes, my passion does have an edge, as it is forthrightness unleashed.*

"I say, 'If you aren't willing to help me, or let me help you, then at least get out of my way.' When you invoke me, get ready for unbridled action. It may feel like I push you along too fast, and it may feel unsafe. But I assure you that I'm simply helping you through doors that open so that we can proceed as light-beings. We have much catching up [with the mission] *to do, and dilly-dallying only further thwarts our efforts.*

"Do not procrastinate, delay, or fear the change that always accompanies action and moving forward. Do not be afraid of making the wrong decision; rather, fear living in indecision. I am Kali, single-minded focus mixed with fiery passion and deep caring about many causes."

Kali told me that she, like a lot of women, has been called a "bitch," when she's simply being powerful and unwavering.

Helps with:

- Courage
- Determination
- Direction
- Focus
- Motivation
- Protection
- Tenacity

INVOCATION

Kali comes immediately if you think of her name: "Kali, Kali, Kali." She arrives like a sudden and powerful rainstorm, with purpose and determination. She's excellent at extracting the heart of the problem from any situation presented to her. So, if you tell her that you want help with your love life, for example, Kali will see the true underlying issues. She'll give you very clear, forceful direction, without mincing any words.

Krishna
(Hindu; India)

Also known as *The Divine One.*

The Hindu Trinity includes Brahma, Shiva, and Vishnu, the three gods who create, protect, and oversee the life cycles on Earth. The god Vishnu incarnates whenever he's needed in physical form to overcome inhumane practices. Krishna is the eighth incarnation (also called an *avatar*) of Vishnu.

Krishna incarnated at midnight on the eighth day of the season of *Bhadrapada* (the Hindu word for "late summer") sometime between 3200 and 3100 B.C. He delivered the Hindu spiritual text, the Bhagavad Gita. Today, Krishna is one of India's most popular deities.

Krishna's legends portray him as a romantic figure, and many paintings show him and his partner, Radha (one of the goddess Lakshmi's incarnations) exhibiting beautiful romantic love. Some Feng Shui experts recommend placing a picture of Krishna and Radha in the romance corner* of your home to manifest a soulmate relationship.

Krishna is a deliverer of joy and happiness. When you call upon him, you'll likely feel a swelling of warm, loving energy in your heart and belly. He says, *"Never underestimate the healing power of love. Its depths are further than the reaches of any ocean, and there is no barrier that it cannot overcome. Use this power within your mind that is everlasting, with no need to hold back, as it's a constantly renewable resource to use again and again. Pour love over every situation, and watch the rewards you will reap!"*

Helps with:

- Blessings
- Food, purifying and spiritualizing
- Gardening, crops, and flowers
- Joy
- Relationships
- Romantic love
- Spiritual awakening
- Vegetarianism

INVOCATION

Krishna loves to connect with people through the offering of, and blessing of, food. Prior to eating something, look at the food and mentally call upon Krishna. Tell him that the food is your offering to him. As he accepts your gift, he will bless and purify the food with his highly spiritualized energy. Thank him, and then completely ingest his blessings by eating the food slowly, enjoying each bite completely. Have a mental conversation with him while you're eating this food. You'll notice that the experience is like being with a very wise dining companion who offers you stellar wisdom and sage advice.

---

* For those of you unfamiliar with Feng Shui, it is the ancient Chinese art of placement. As part of Feng Shui practice, one is directed to situate certain items in specific areas of one's domicile in order to effect a certain goal. For example, if you wish to find a soulmate, you would place objects that symbolize love in the "romance corner"—usually the far right quadrant of one's home. For more information, please consult Terah Kathryn Collins's book *The Western Guide to Feng Shui* (Hay House, 1996).

Kuan Ti
(China)

Also known as *Kuan Jung, Kuan Yu.*

Kuan Ti is the Chinese warrior god who acts to prevent war. He's a prophet who predicts the future, and he protects people from lower spirits.

In his human incarnation, Kuan Ti was a Chinese war hero and Han dynasty general, well known for his warriorlike skills and intelligent decisions. When he passed away, he was elevated to the status of god. He works arm-in-arm with Archangel Michael on matters of justice within government systems.

He says, *"The men who are in positions of power are playing a dangerous game with their saber-rattling. It will backfire and explode into wars of dangerous proportions if this high drama isn't curtailed. It's all a game of power that they play, but of the most explosive kind. The populace must intervene and demand peaceful methods, rather than these dangerous ploys to capture control and coin. I will intervene along with you, as we replace our fear-based leaders with those who act from wisdom and understanding. It's the only way."*

While I was sitting in a bird aviary in China, I mentally asked Kuan Ti advice on avoiding wars and manifesting world peace. He replied with powerful energy: *"Inner soldiers are needed at this time—those who will march to their inner commander in spiritual terms. Those who will carry out their inner commander's marching orders and who do not worry about reprimands from the outside world. The only authority figure requiring your obedience is the mighty General within. In this respect, truth shall prevail, and peace upon this planet is possible once again."*

Helps with:

- Justice and freedom for falsely accused prisoners and prisoners-of-war
- Legal matters
- Prophecies about world events
- Psychic abilities, increasing accuracy and details of
- Space clearing
- Spirit releasement
- War, preventing and ending

INVOCATION

Call upon Kuan Ti if you're concerned about world events, especially those involving warfare. Mentally say:

"Kuan Ti, I ask for your intervention, wisdom, and council about [describe the situation to him]. Thank you for intervening and bringing about a peaceful resolution through wisdom and understanding. Thank you for assisting and counseling the leaders involved, and helping them use their power in wise ways for the benefit of all."

Kuan Yin
(Asia)

Also known as *Kwan Yin, Quan Yin, Guanyin,
Quan'Am, Kannon, Kanin, Kwannon.*

Kuan Yin is one of the most beloved and popular Eastern divinities. A physically and spiritually beautiful Chinese goddess of mercy, compassion, and protection, her name means "she who hears prayers." Kuan Yin does, in fact, hear and answer every prayer sent her way.

Kuan Yin is both a goddess and a *bodhisattva,* which means "enlightened being." Bodhisattvas can become Buddhas; however, Kuan Yin has such a deep love for humanity that after she attained enlightenment, instead of ascending to Buddhahood, she chose to remain in human form until every one of us becomes enlightened. She's devoted to helping us fully open up to our spiritual gifts, attain profound knowledge and enlightenment, and reduce world suffering. It's said that the mere uttering of her name affords guaranteed protection from harm.

Kuan Yin is often called "the Mother Mary of the East," because she represents feminine divinity and goddess energy in the Buddhist religion, in the same way that Mary radiates sweet loving femininity within Christianity. Kuan Yin teaches us to practice a life of harmlessness, using great care to ease suffering in the world and not add to it in any way. You may see the color red when she's around, such as red sparkles of light or a red mist that appears from out of nowhere.

A woman named Mary Urssing told me this beautiful story of her interactions with Kuan Yin:

"I was in Hawaii and had just purchased a crystal pendant depicting Kuan Yin. Right after donning the necklace, I started to hear her talk to me in a soft, soothing Asian voice. On the last morning of my vacation, I was awakened by Kuan Yin telling me to go outside for a walk. I sat on our porch but was urged to walk. I did just that, carrying a portable cassette recorder with headphones, through which I heard beautiful Hawaiian music. I noticed a plumeria flower on the ground that was pink, to me a sign of love. I would normally pick these flowers and immediately put them in my hair, but things were different today. I just held the flower.

"As I neared a waterfall, I heard Kuan Yin tell me that I was to have an initiation of self-passion, far beyond self-love. The moment was very sacred, as I knew that I was taking a vow that was more intense than anything I'd ever done. I accepted, and was told to stand inside the waterfall in a cove, a cocoon of sorts. I was to really be, feel, and know self-love. I felt this with all of me and grounded this moment into my complete being. Trying now to put it into words doesn't seem to do justice to this personal ceremony.

"As I took in this energy, I was asked to seal it with the symbol that I unknowingly had chosen for this time—the plumeria. As I threw my flower into the waterfall to ritualize my ceremony, I saw it sink, and as it did, the water in its place turned the most beautiful color of deep, passionate red. I actually saw the water turn red! All of this instantly changed me, and I knew that it was time to honor myself and my power.

"Later that day, I told my friend Marlies that I'd had the most amazing experience at a waterfall. She asked, 'Was it at Kuan Yin's waterfall?' I was surprised by her question and asked her for more information. She explained that Kuan Yin's statue was in one of the waterfalls on the island. Sure enough, as I scouted around later that day, there it was—a beautiful statue of Kuan Yin tucked away on a stone shelf in the cove of the waterfall. She had called me to her sanctuary!"

In Kona, Hawaii, there are many beautiful statues of Kuan Yin. Near one statue that depicts her holding a lotus flower, she said this to me: *"Here are my sacred instructions: First, have mercy upon yourselves. You have endured much in your land, and you have eons of lessons yet before you. Only through a gentle touch is Nirvana revealed. Stretch and reach for greatness, but always with a gentle approach. Seek not opportunities, but allow them to gently come to you as a lotus flower floats upon the currents of water amidst a gentle breeze. Strive, but not with hurry—enjoy the process upon which you embark. Know that each step along the way is akin to a party—a celebration of movement, which is itself a miracle.*

"Appreciate the godliness within yourself, within each of you. Do not chide yourself for your errors and mistakes, but laugh, grow, and learn from them instead. You, my gentle child, are doing just fine—in fact, very well indeed.

"If I were to give you any word of wisdom, it would be the word that best embodies love upon this Earth plane to me: compassion. Growing past all shame and embarrassment, and moving toward appreciation, not just for the 'good' parts of yourself and others, but for all along the way—it's all good, believe me. And if you can know that as the eternal truth sooner rather than later, your happiness will come galloping toward you at the speed of mustangs with winged hooves. Believe that as the truth. Now.

"Wisdom comes from sitting still and listening, not from rushing to get ahead. A still heart receives love and information more readily than one that is harried. Do something simple today: Pick a flower and simply study it with no intent. Be blank. Be open. And know that whatever comes to you is good, and a lesson in the making—always and forever."

Helps with:

- Clairvoyance
- Compassion
- Feminine grace, beauty, and power
- Kindness, gentleness, and sweetness, toward self and others
- Love, receiving and giving
- Mercy
- Musical abilities, developing (especially singing)
- Protection—especially for women and children
- Spiritual enlightenment and gifts

INVOCATION

Kuan Yin always hears and answers our prayers, and no special ritual is necessary to contact her. However, you may feel a more heart-centered connection with her through the use of flowers. For instance, hold a blossom, gaze at a budding plant or bouquet, or draw or look at a picture of flowers. Those who work closely with Kuan Yin often chant the mantra: *Om Mani Padme Hum,* which means "Hail to the jewel in the lotus flower."

One prayer that will help you invoke Kuan Yin is:

"Beloved Kuan Yin, please hear the prayers within my heart. Please uncover and understand what my true needs are. I ask for your intervention into the areas of my life that are triggering pain. Please come to my aid and assistance, guiding me to see my situation in a new light of love and compassion. Please help me to be like you and live peacefully and purposefully."

Kuthumi
(Sikh; Theosophy; New Age)
❧❧

Also known as *Mahatma Kuthumi mal Singh, Koot Hoomi,*
Sirdar Thakar Singh Sadhanwalia, K.H.

Kuthumi is a pseudonym for a Sikh spiritual leader who lived in the
1800s named Sirdar Thakar Singh Sadhanwali, according to
Theosophical researchers (including author K. Paul Johnson).

Madame Blavatsky met Singh during her extensive travels in India.
This is also when she met and studied under the Eastern Indian spiritual teachers who would be the basis for Djwhal Khul, Master Hillarion,
and El Morya, whom she referred to as "the Mahatmas." Blavatsky pro-
moted these men's spiritual teachings in North America, protecting their
true identities with pseudonyms. She would produce letters from Singh
and the other Mahatmas, sometimes claiming that the letters materialized from the ethers.

When the men passed over, Blavatsky and her followers (most
notably Alice Bailey and Elizabeth Clare Prophet) began channeling
messages from them. This was the first usage of the term "ascended masters." According to the "new" Theosophists, Kuthumi's past lives include
Saint Francis and Pythagoras.

When I called upon Kuthumi, he came to me dressed as a circus
clown! He said, *"Life is a three-ring circus, and the key is to not let yourself*
get distracted by events around you. Steady focus and a willingness to search

for higher truth will move your consciousness away from anxiety and instill it with peace.

"Refuse to be distracted or thwarted. Use your stubbornness rightly by concentrating only upon that which is good—in that way, you truly overcome evil in every sense of the word. Allow me to show you ways to access the reaches of the higher dimensions where peace is accessible to all. Above the din of the Earth plane, we reach Nirvana together, singly, yet side-by-side. The holiest prospect is teaching peace through self-attainment."

Helps with:

- Dedication to life purpose
- Focus

INVOCATION

If you find yourself distracted from your major goals and life purpose, ask Kuthumi to help you maintain diligence when it comes to your priorities. He'll help you organize your schedule in a balanced way. Ask him for help anytime you feel overwhelmed by multiple tasks:

"Dearest Kuthumi, I ask for your intervention. Please remove all distractions from my mind and schedule, allowing me to focus completely on my true life's purpose. Please let any life changes occur gently and peacefully, and help me notice my spiritual guidance and Divine will. I now release to you any ego-based fears that would deter me from my path. Help me recognize when I procrastinate with respect to my purpose so that I may be fully immersed in the joy of spiritual service."

Lakshmi
(Buddhist, Hindu, India, Jain)

Also known as *Haripriya, Jaganmatri, Laxmi, Matrirupa, Vriddhi.*

Lakshmi's name is derived from the Sanskrit word *Laksya,* which means "goal" or "aim."

Lakshmi is a beautiful, golden-skinned moon goddess of prosperity and good fortune who brings blessings of abundance to everyone. Lakshmi also represents beauty, purity, generosity, and true happiness. It's said that she sprang forth from the churning ocean bearing gifts and lotus flowers, looking so beautiful that all of the gods immediately wanted her as their wife. She chose to be with the sun god, Vishnu. She was thereafter reborn as Vishnu's companion in each of his lives.

Because Lakshmi's true mission is to bring eternal happiness to Earth, she helps us find meaningful careers that bring about handsome rewards, including personal fulfillment. She knows that wealth, in and of itself, isn't enough to create lasting happiness—it must be accompanied by spirituality and a feeling of accomplishment. So Lakshmi may lead us to our life's work, which will create joy and abundance for ourselves and others.

Lakshmi is associated with lotus flowers. Some legends say that she was born from, and lives in, one of these blossoms. In artwork, she's usually depicted carrying, or standing upon, a lotus, which is a symbol of spiritual awakening and peace.

Lakshmi brings grace, beauty, and love into homes, and ensures that all household needs are met. She's adored by Ganesh, and they often work together to help people meet their goals.

Lakshmi speaks in a sweet, melodious voice and says, *"The attainment of wealth is one of life's greatest mysteries and challenges. Most spiritual aspirants abhor the pursuit of money, yet they long for the freedom and services that it affords. Many of your spiritual teachers and healers are conflicted about accepting money for their work, yet they long for the day when they can quit other forms of employment and devote themselves fully to the service of spirituality.*

"This dilemma must be dealt with, for we here in the strata you call 'Heaven' see many solutions at hand, most of which we can help you with, without your needing to strain or think so much. This, I will tell you: Pressing with your mind to try to make things happen is your greatest barrier and blockage, which can only be overcome when you become convinced that all riches worth having are already manifested within. When you relax with this knowledge and know with certainty that all is taken care of, then all restrictions are lifted completely."

Helps with:

- Abundance
- Beauty and aesthetics
- Happiness, lasting
- Home supplies and food, manifesting
- Space clearing for the home

INVOCATION

Lakshmi loves a grateful and appreciative heart. So as you call upon her, imagine that all of your wishes have been granted in a Divine way. Feel grateful that this is so. Know that the power of your Creator, combined with your faith and Lakshmi's loving help, manifests into form miraculously. Her manifestations are the physical embodiment of the love and gratitude that you now feel.

Stay focused on your desires, seeing and feeling them as being already manifested. Then give thanks to Lakshmi by mentally chanting: *"Om Nameh Lakshmi Namah,"* which is a prayer of thanks and reverence.

Lugh
(Celtic)

Also known as *Lug, Lugus, Lleu.*

Lugh is a youthful sun god with a magical hound, helmet, and spear that completely protect him and all who call upon him. Lugh helps humans develop their inner sorcerer or sorceress with Divine love. He's also associated with fertility and yielding a bountiful summer harvest.

Legends say that Lugh was a master craftsman, poet, healer, and jack-of-all-trades, and that there was no skill that he couldn't perform.

When I called upon Lugh to provide me with a message for this book, a breathtakingly handsome man with a helmet and shield appeared before me, with a Roman look to his dress. He said, *"You called? What can I help you with?"* When I described a particular situation that I could use his assistance with, Lugh said, *"Just a minute— something is brewing here. I'll check into it and be right back."*

He then returned a fraction of a moment later, carrying some sort of potion. It looked like a blue powder glistening with a liquidlike sheen. Lugh said, *"This is based upon my assessment of your inner yearnings, leanings, and tendencies."* He very politely asked if he could anoint me with the healing potion that he explained was custom-made for the situation. He added that he tailor-made all of his magical recipes for each individual and their particular situation.

I lay back, and Lugh swept the hair off my forehead. He seemed to brush my aura there as well. He asked me to remove my sunglasses so that he could freely anoint me. He pinched some of the powder and drizzled it on my forehead, then spread generous portions all over the top of my head and face, covering me like a skullcap.

He asked me to breathe in the essence very deeply, and then he said, *"This potion is infused with magical properties that will help support the resolution of this problem, in much the same way that vitamins infuse you with energy and help you have a strong workout at the gym. The vitamins lift you up, but it's still up to you to go to the gym and do the work. In the same vein, allow my apothecary potion to support your efforts, boost your faith and confidence, and bring you all the way back home centered in peace and joy."* Then he closed his healing ceremony with me by saying, *"All my love!"* and disappeared.

Helps with:

- Alchemy
- Artistic projects—including art, crafts, poetry, and music
- Divine magic
- Healing from painful situations
- Protection of all kinds
- Solutions to any problem

INVOCATION

Lugh is a powerful force who will come quickly when called. Think of his name and feel the strength, power, and magnitude of his energy. Then, tell him about your needs and the issues that you request help with. As described above, he may leave for a moment to retrieve a healing balm or potion. Give him as much time as he needs to address your situation fully. You'll know when he's finished with his treatment because his energy will withdraw until you next call upon him.

Send him your thank-yous, and know that he receives them gratefully. Lugh will watch over the progress of your situation, all the way to completion, so feel free to call upon him anytime during the process of resolution.

Lu-Hsing
(China)

Also known as *Pinyin Lu Xing*.

Lu-Hsing is the god of salaries, pay, success, career progress, investments, steady accumulation, wealth, and employees. He's one of three Chinese stellar deities known collectively as "the Fu Lu Shou San Hsing," the gods who bring about happiness, fortune, wealth, and longevity.

Lu-Hsing was a mortal man named Shih Fen who was a high-ranking royal court official in the 2nd-century B.C. He was deified following his death. Lu-Hsing takes note of, and rewards, those who are committed and dedicated to their careers. He warns against engaging in corrupt behavior to get ahead. Lu-Hsing suggests healing unpleasant or dishonest situations through prayer, and by seeking Divine guidance first, before taking more drastic action such as calling the corruption to the attention of others.

Invoke Lu-Hsing before a job search so that doors will open to you easily, leading to the high road of your chosen profession. But be aware that Lu-Hsing's signs telling you which doors to walk through can be quite subtle. It takes an agile mind and much alertness to properly heed his guidance. Those who receive his counseling will appreciate the dry wit that he exhibits and the twists and turns he orchestrates, which seem to be part of his modus operandi. Always invoke Lu-Hsing before asking your boss for a raise or promotion.

"Do not rest on your laurels," he cautions. If you want to enjoy your current success instead of worrying about how to climb the next mountain, you'll need to tell Lu-Hsing that you want to pause for a regrouping.

I invoked Lu-Hsing during a visit to China, and I asked him to address the topic of attaining financial security and success. He said, *"The secret of financial success is the willingness to adopt a warrior spirit in attitude, grace, and presence. This does not mean adopting an air of aggressiveness, but rather, a spirit of making treaties and pacts with oneself and others.*

"Warriors have an outlook of expecting a positive outcome, and a willingness to do whatever is needed to incur that outcome. It means not giving up, but allowing for flexibility, and to flow with the energy or chi as it moves along. Be strong, be vigilant for success, and be sensitive to the energy undercurrents, and you shan't go wrong."

Helps with:

- Employment, all aspects of
- Job interviews
- Raises and promotions

INVOCATION

Call upon Lu-Hsing before any major event involving employment. Imagine that you're having a mental meeting with him and that Lu-Hsing is the ultimate executive who will clear the way for whatever you request. Visualize him taking notes during your discussion, and know that he'll take care of everything. Ask him to give you very clear guidance that you'll easily understand. Then, write, "Thank you, Lu-Hsing" on a piece of paper, fold it, and hold it in your palm during the applicable situation—whether it's asking your boss for a raise, getting through a job interview, or taking part in an important meeting.

Maat
(Egypt)

Also known as *Ma'at, Maa, Maet, Maht, Mat, Maut.*

The Egyptian goddess of truth, fairness, and justice, Maat is the daughter of the sun god, Ra, and consort/wife of the magical scribe god, Thoth. Legend says that when Ra created the world, he created his daughter to be the embodiment of integrity.

Maat is the goddess of fairness, integrity, promises, truth, and justice. Her symbol is the feather, which she uses with a scale of justice to weigh the heaviness of guilt or deceit within a newly deceased soul's heart.

She has impeccable abilities to discern true character, honesty, and motives in people. Invoke Maat to keep dishonest individuals and situations away from you, and for protection against dark or lower energies. If Maat deems your motives to be pure, she'll treat you with the warmest love. If not, then she may put you through trials of purification—or you can engage in rituals, lifestyle changes, affirmations, and ceremonies to avert her trials and bring you her comradeship. She doesn't judge; she's truth itself. Maat also oversees legal matters to ensure harmony and honesty.

She says, *"Everyone possesses magical abilities, and for a younger woman, the key lies in being very attuned to her menstrual cycle. As she practices building greater harmony with the cycles of the moon and realizes their connection to her flow, she will become 'moon-struck' and open herself to a* shift that unleashes practical and esoteric abilities—both of which will create in her a beautiful confidence only seen in great displays of feminine energy. The big cats, for instance, are unapologetic about their power. They're enchanting because they put their full force in each step.

"For men and women who are not of childbearing age, the cycles of the moon do not have such obvious marks, yet we're all still affected. Anyone—even spirits—within the gravitational pull of this planet will feel the sway that the moon creates."

"Pay exquisitely close attention to your relationship with the moon, this great source of light. Visit her often. You will find her to be a source of magical abilities that will give you important messages."

Helps with:

- Addictions and cravings, overcoming
- Clarification in confusing situations
- Discerning the truth, and integrity in others
- Divine magic
- Integrity and commitments—for oneself and others
- Orderliness
- Protection against deceit and manipulation
- Purifying the body

INVOCATION

If you're confused or undecided about a situation, ask Maat to help you clarify your true feelings and intentions. She'll give you insight into the other people involved in the situation as well. Before you call upon her, though, be absolutely certain that you're willing to face the truth and possibly receive information that you don't want to know (such as being told about someone's lack of integrity, for example).

When you're ready to work with Maat, show her respect by sitting upright. Then say:

"Beloved and Powerful Maat, please come to me now. You are the shower of truth and integrity, and I need you to shine your light upon [describe the situation or name the person involved]. Please shine the light of truth onto my mind and heart, helping me feel and know its wisdom. Please help me release any narrow thinking that could blind me to the facts, and help me use the truth as the foundation for all actions. Thank you."

Maeve
(Ireland)

Also known as *Mab, Medb, Medhbh, Madb, Queen of Connacht.*

A powerful warrior goddess whose name means "intoxicated woman," Maeve is renowned for her strong will and her ability to manifest whatever and whomever she wants. She's associated with the menstrual cycle and feminine beauty. Maeve is also a fairy queen and land goddess who is loved by horses.

Call upon Maeve anytime you need guidance about natural and alternative healing methods. For instance, when you're in a health-food store, ask Maeve to guide you to vitamins, minerals, herbs, and oils to help with whatever situation you need assistance with. Like a friendly and wise shopping companion, Maeve will steer you to the right products or books to use.

I spoke with her near a river laced with fragrant flowers outside Dublin, Ireland. The area was rich with beautiful fairies who were tending to the flowers. Maeve came quickly when I called her, and she told me:

"I oversee the magical kingdom of the fae. I'm not one of the fairy folk, but I delight and am invoked in their Divine plan and mission. Therefore, when you call upon them, you likely also call upon me. My mission is to be a leader, and to untwist spells so that they can be purified and centered before their delivery to the fairy folk. You might say that I'm a mediator or

translator between them and yourselves, making sure that the wishes they grant you are of the highest value.

"Unlike the angels on-high, the fairy folk live in more of a time density and must use their time wisely. So must you! You can ask me to ferret out your material wishes, as I'm also keen to provide for you in the highest way. Yet I help you avoid possessions that would in fact 'keep' you and require such high maintenance as to distract you from your lighted pathway.

"I'm especially fond of the healers among you, and must admit a special penchant for the youth involved in healing ambitions. Ask me for advice on herbal alchemy, potions, oils, and elixirs. I infuse them with magical energies of the highest caliber!"

Helps with:

- Alchemy
- Aromatherapy
- Elementals, connecting with (especially the fairies)
- Feminine beauty, strength, and attractiveness
- Healers, beginning practitioners, students of healing, or would-be healers
- Herbology
- Horses, healing and protecting
- Menstrual cycles

INVOCATION

Maeve comes whenever or wherever she's needed; however, you may find that your initial conversations with her are clearer and easier to discern if you begin speaking with her outside in nature, especially where flowers grow freely. Look at a flower and imagine the fairies flitting in and out of the petals, tending them with joy and love. Then mentally say:

"Queen Maeve, it is I [state your name]. I'd like to get to know you, and I respectfully ask for your mentorship in my healing work and on my spiritual path. I'm sincerely dedicated to healing, and I promise to continue taking good care of the environment. I'm willing to help in your mission of world healing, and ask that you take me under your powerful wings and guide me clearly and powerfully. Thank you for opening doors to my healing work and career."

Maitreya
(Buddhist; Chinese; New Age)

Also known as *Buddha of the Future; Future Buddha; Lord Maitreya, Lord Maitreya Maitri, Happy Buddha, Hotei, Laughing Buddha, Maitreya Buddha, Miroku-Bosatsu.*

Historians disagree about Maitreya's history. Many scholars believe that he was a monk named Sthiramati who showed great compassion and kindness toward others. It's said that Sthiramati was so committed to bringing about happiness that he was bestowed the name Maitreya, which means "the loving one."

However, he's sometimes called Hotei, who was a T'ang Dynasty monk renowned for giving candy to children. Chinese Buddhists believe that Hotei was one of Maitreya's incarnations. Others believe that Maitreya incarnated during the time of Krishna as the famous Rishi written of in the Vedas, and also during the time of Goutama Buddha's Earth life.

In some Buddhist populations, it's believed that Maitreya is the *bodhisattva* (enlightened one) who is successor to Goutama Siddhartha as the next Buddha. He's often portrayed as a smiling Buddha with a protruding belly, called "the Laughing Buddha."

It's prophesied that between 4- and 5,000 years after Goutama Buddha left his physical body, Maitreya will reappear on Earth in human form when Buddhism needs reigniting. Maitreya will then teach and lead people through example, and eventually replace Goutama Buddha as *the* Buddha.

In New Age circles, he's called Lord Maitreya, and he's viewed as a member of the Great White Brotherhood, along with Jesus, Saint-Germain, and Archangel Michael. He's said to be a master of the sixth ray of light of enlightenment and ascension.

I spoke with Maitreya while seated in front of a large Laughing Buddha statue, which seemed to become animated as soon as I mentally began talking with him. A friend of mine, Lynnette Brown, was seated next to me and also heard similar messages from him and saw him move and speak.

Maitreya said, *"Laughter is sacred. Laugh more, play more, and sing more to harmonize yourself with the natural world. Even humming moves your vibrational chord outward to mesh with the universe and all of humanity. Music is a gift bestowed upon all of us, from the Allness. Nirvana itself is a song, a dance, and a play. Delight in the unfoldment of this great musical that you call 'life.' And call upon your enlightenment, not through striving, but on the wings of laughter and song.*

"There will come a day when joy will reign once again. Nirvana is joy and carefree laughter. When you laugh, you're most connected to the Infinite, because the breath emitted through laughter is the Allness. A heart filled with gaiety, mirth, playfulness, and laughter is a heart filled with Nirvana-essence. Be childlike eternally, Beloved Being, and worry not about your ancestors or of creation—it in itself is locked in a tight chamber of safety that nothing can permeate or destroy. Life itself is eternal, and an unfoldment of joy.

"By centering your mind on the intention of enjoying yourself, you are centered in the moment, and thus you capture the full flavor of that moment as deliciously as sweet, juicy fruit. Savor its delectable sensations and all of its variety, for life is a banquet and a feast. And just as in a buffet, where you must try various platters to attain the experience that teaches you your likes and dislikes, so must you also gain knowledge through a wide range of experiences. And thus you can be selective as to that which you place on your platter and partake into your belly. Enjoy the process, and be unafraid to taste and sample new selections put before you.

"Laughter truly is the best medicine of all—you take yourselves far too

seriously, and in so doing, you edge out the secret of harmony on your plan-et: living in joy. Today, seek out ten people who are not smiling, and go out of your way to put a smile on their face. In that way, you will have lit ten candles of light amid darkness."

Helps with:

- Joy
- Laughter and a sense of humor
- Lovingness
- Peace, global and personal

INVOCATION

Imagine, or look at, a picture of the Laughing Buddha—with his huge smile, arms extended joyfully upward, and his large belly protrud-ing. His whole manner exudes the complete release and bliss of a good laugh. Imagine yourself rubbing his belly, and feel how "contagious" his laughter and joy are! Perhaps you'll notice yourself smiling, giggling, or even laughing out loud. Notice how your heart fills with warm love, peace, and utter security.

Mentally tell Maitreya about any situation or relationship that trou-bles you, and notice how he helps you release anxiety. He vows to inter-vene if you promise to continually monitor yourself for worry, and immediately give all of your concerns to him. Feel the weight lifted from your shoulders, and know that there's nothing to fear.

After spending time with Maitreya, watch a funny movie, read a humorous book, or swap silly stories with a friend. The point is to fully release the situation to him through the follow-up process of engaging in play, laughter, and comedy.

Mary, the Beloved Mother
(Judeo-Christian, Catholic)

Also known as *Mother Mary, Our Lady of Guadalupe, Virgin Mary, Queen of the Angels.*

Mary's historical data isn't well known, as the four Gospels that describe her don't go into much detail. Other documents about Mary, such as the *Proto-Evangelion of James,* discuss her birth, childhood, and adulthood—however, scholars can't agree on the validity of such texts. And then there are the New Age books, which provide information about Mary's life based on channeled or regressed information.

The Gospels say that Mary lived her life in Nazareth, which was a small working-class village. She lived with her husband, Joseph; her son, Jesus; and—according to historians—Joseph's four sons and one daughter from his first marriage. Because Joseph worked outside the home as a carpenter or furniture maker, Mary likely spent most of her time tending to family and household needs. Most women in Mary's time didn't receive any education or literacy training. Historians and religious scholars speculate that Mary led a difficult life, struggling to raise enough money for food and taxes, and trying to avoid the dangers of ongoing military and political uprisings.

New Age authors speculate that Mary may have taken baby Jesus to Qumran and temporarily lived among the Essenes, where they both learned the mystical secrets of the Dead Sea Scrolls. They also hypothesize that the brothers and sisters in the household were also offspring of Mary and Joseph.

Many modern-day people, especially children, have seen visions of Mother Mary in places such as Fatima, Lourdes, and Guadalupe. Mary's apparitions and the messages that she delivers to those who see her help us recognize the presence of miraculous masters among us.

Mary has been called "the Queen of the Angels," and her famous interactions with Archangel Gabriel during the annunciation certainly herald this title. Her present persona, too, is definitively angelic: She's among the most loving, patient, and kind of the ascended masters. The angels love her, and they work with her to effect miracles. Yet, behind her gentleness, there's a firm "mother bear" who lovingly warns us to shape up.

Mary is especially concerned with children, and she counsels us to use wisdom, intelligence, and love in our parenting decisions. She's especially watchful of the new "Indigo and Crystal Children," who bring gifts of salvation to the planet. Mary will assist anyone whose life purpose involves helping these young ones, and she will open doors to child advocates. She helps those whose intentions are benevolent toward children, including those who seek to abolish chemicals that harm children's psyches, including dietary pesticides and additives, and psychoactive medications such as Ritalin.

A woman named Mary Frances sent me this story explaining how Mary helped her and her children:

"I was 39, pregnant, and quite large. My daughter was seven years old. We were taking care of a friend's daughters on this day and decided to drive to the coast to gather seashells. We drove the car into a very sandy lot, parked, and enjoyed the day at the beach. Then we all got into the car, and lo and behold, we couldn't get out of the deep sand. The wheels of the car were stuck. We all got out to see if the car would move without our weight in it, but it wouldn't. Nothing seemed to work. We were stuck, and all alone in a very isolated location!

"My daughter began crying and praying aloud. She said,

'Oh, dear Virgin, you've said that we should call you anytime we need your help. We're stuck in the sand, my mother is pregnant, and I can't push the car as I'm too small. Please, please, please.' The other two girls laughed and asked me, 'Does she really believe this?' I answered, 'Of course she does!'

"It was getting dark, though, and we all began to worry— when from out of nowhere, a pickup truck with three men came into view. The men stopped and pushed us out of the sand, and we were on our way in no time. I couldn't help but look at my friend's daughters and say, 'See?!'"

I frequently call upon Mary for help with healings and guidance, and I always find that she fills my heart with the sweetest warmth and love. I recently asked Mary for a message when I visited a shrine dedicated to her at the magnificent (circa 1200) cathedral in Cologne. My lower back felt stiff and sore from traveling, so I also lit a white candle in front of her statue and asked her for a healing. My candle joined dozens of others in a beautiful ceremony of lighted prayers.

I knew that Mary was with me when I felt her familiar calling card of loving warmth in my heart. The warmth encompassed my entire chest and stomach and caused my breath to deepen.

"*Compassion,*" she repeated swiftly in one of my ears in the sweetest voice—like the music of the wind blowing through springtime leaves. "*Compassion is what the world hungers for most, which means love coupled with an understanding of the other person's point of view and feelings.*

"*So much strife stems from an aggressive desire for compassion—a desire to force the other parties involved to agree with you, because everyone is too afraid to admit that they can see and understand why the other acts in this way. Throw down your arms and come to me for a reuniting with all others. Throw your arms around me and feel my embrace! Allow me to soothe shattered nerves and hurt feelings.*

"*Come to me, those of you who are afraid. I shall help you rise above all strain and suffering so that you may see the unlimited viewpoint of all others. You will see that those whom you fear or resent are merely children who are afraid, too.*

"Lay down your arms, humanity. You are weary from constantly defending yourselves against imagined dangers that are of your own making. Be unafraid of truth, which overcomes all fear. And the hard and fast truth that never wavers is that your Father loves you eternally. Allow me to pour this love in your direction and cover you with its healing power. You may bathe in this well of Divine love at any time, simply by reconnecting your thoughts to those of God's. How to do that? Through having compassion for yourself and others. If you are unable to reach this state, allow me to assist you. For, like your Father, I shall love you always eternally."

As I stood up and walked out of the cathedral, I no longer felt any back pain.

Helps with:

- Children, adopting
- Children, all other issues related to
- Children, support for those who help
- Fertility
- Healing of all kinds
- Mercy

INVOCATION

Mary comes to anyone who calls upon her, regardless of that person's religion or past behavior. She's all-loving and all-forgiving. When she appears, you may smell fragrant flowers or see sparkles of cornflower-blue lights. You'll feel a sense of peace and safety, as if a powerful and loving mother has just entered a child's bedroom to chase away nightmares and replace them with sweet dreams.

Invoke Mary by imagining or looking at a picture or statue of her, or call upon her aloud or mentally:

"Beloved Mary, Queen of the Angels and Mother of Jesus, I ask for your help. [Describe the issue.] Thank you for showering this situation with your blessings and giving me insight, so I may learn and grow from this experience. Thank you for showing me God's will so that we all may have peace."

Melchizedek

(Judaism; New Age)

Melchizedek's name is said to mean "king of righteousness" or "genuine or rightful king." He was a Canaanite priest-king of Salem (now known as Jerusalem) and was a teacher of Abraham. Ancient mystical texts describe him as one who conducts spirit releasement on a massive scale, working in conjunction with Archangel Michael.

Descriptions of Melchizedek's history are conflicting. In the Dead Sea Scrolls, he's called Michael, and there's some allusion to Melchizedek being one and the same with Archangel Michael and Jesus. This latter speculation is echoed by Apostle Paul's letters to the Hebrews, in which Paul discusses Melchizedek and Jesus as both being great high priests, and that Melchizedek was a foreshadowing to Jesus' appearance on Earth. The Eastern spiritual text *Nag Hammadi* also discusses Melchizedek as being a past incarnation of Jesus Christ.

According to *The Book of Enoch*, Melchizedek was the child of Noah's brother, Nir. Nir's wife died before giving birth, and Melchizedek was delivered posthumously from his mother's womb. However, there's other speculation that he's actually Noah's son Shem.

It is said that Melchizedek made the first offering of bread and wine to Abraham for his military victory. He's even depicted as holding a cup or chalice in a stone sculpture from the Chartres Cathedral in France. Saint Paul spoke of Jesus Christ as a priest according to the order of (or in the succession of) Melchizedek because Jesus later instituted the use of bread and wine in the Eucharistic sacrifice at the Last Supper. The Council of Trent even discussed Melchizedek offering bread and wine, and then Jesus instituting it at the Last Supper.

In New Age circles, Melchizedek is thought of as a group of high-level spiritual beings who are custodians and teachers of ancient esoteric secrets. The group is sometimes called "the Cosmic Priesthood" or "Order of Melchizedek." This group was described in Psalms: *"The Lord has sworn and will not change his mind, you are a priest forever according to the order of Melchizedek."*

When I called upon Melchizedek, an extremely tall man with piercing blue eyes appeared before me. He showed me that he oversees a switching station into which stream various colors of the rainbow. These hues are the energies of universal vibrations, given off by everything: the planets and stars; organizations; and thoughts and emotions.

Melchizedek said: *"I am part of the regulating program that balances and harmonizes all energies. These energies are flowing continuously, and they form the basic structure of the universe. All substances are formulated from these agents. All atomic particles revolve around them, too. So, to rearrange the substance of some situation, you must call upon the internal colors to rearrange it so that differing amounts of those colors exist, and the order in which they appear is changed.*

"A reduction in red essence, for instance, reduces the pain threshold. As the tolerance for pain is reduced, the situation must become softer and gentler. The formulas for re-creating situations using the colors are a sacred science that is very complex. It's probably best for you to involve my organization in the process. We operate on the Law of Noninterference with your Earth operations. However, we do make ourselves readily available to those who direct their attention toward us and pose requests for our assistance."

Melchizedek showed me how his regulatory system could instantly rearrange and reorganize matter by remixing its energy color components. This could be used to undo a negative situation, to increase flow and supply, and to create or attract new substances or situations.

Helps with:

- Correcting an unpleasant situation
- Esoteric understanding
- Manifestation
- Purification
- Shielding against psychic attack
- Spirit releasement
- Therapy involving colors (that is, Aura-Soma, chakra clearing, crystals, Feng Shui, Reiki, etc.)

INVOCATION

"Wisdom of Melchizedek, power of Melchizedek, order of Melchizedek, I invite and invoke your presence and protection. Melchizedek, thank you for clearing away all lower energies thoroughly! Melchizedek, thank you for purifying me and this situation. Melchizedek, thank you for rearranging this situation so that it reflects only the highest spiritual laws and energies. Divine wisdom, power, and order now guide my actions, thoughts, and words; and I am safe and protected in all ways."

Merlin
(Celtic; United Kingdom)

Also known as *Merddin, Myrddin, Merlyn, Emrys*.

A controversial figure—did he really live, or was he merely a legend?—Merlin represents the great old sage-wizard archetype. He's known as a powerful magician, a spiritual teacher, and a psychic visionary who helped King Arthur during fifth-century Camelot in Wales. He's associated with the goddesses of Avalon and Glastonbury, including Viviane, Guinevere, and The Lady of the Lake.

Those who question his reality as an actual human being say that Merlin may have been based upon an ancient Druid mystic. In any event, biographical information about him is seemingly nonexistent. However, many divinities didn't lead physical lives, but they're still quite powerful and real among us in the spirit world. Merlin is one of them. Although some New Age philosophers argue that Merlin was an early incarnation of Saint-Germain, I and many of the peers whom I respect have interacted with Merlin's spirit as a personality quite distinct and apart from Saint-Germain.

Merlin is happy to give lightworkers a magical leg-up; however, he always cautions that we use our "inner wizards" in the name of spiritual service and not for self-gain.

I thought it was fitting to ask Merlin to speak to readers of this book while I sat at the Stonehenge circle in England. He said, *"Welcome to the*

Mystery School, where both dark and bright mysteries reside together. I'm the champion of both dark and light, recognizing the power within both forces if they're approached fearlessly, but with uncompromising respect for their force. If it's an increase in magical knowledge, spell-casting, or inner strength or power that you seek, by all means call upon me. I'm pleased to teach and guide, but be aware that I'm perceived as a powerful taskmaster, one who doesn't take lightly to gluttony or indolence. Be prepared to work hard without compromise when you invoke me."

Helps with:

- Alchemy
- Crystals
- Divine magic
- Energy work and healing
- Prophecy and divination
- Psychic abilities
- Shape-shifting
- Time-warping

INVOCATION

During his mortal lifetime, Merlin rarely spent time indoors. He frequently left Camelot to meditate by himself in the forest, and only went back when he was called upon by Arthur and others for assistance. For this reason, it's best to invoke Merlin when you're outside, especially among trees.

Before you even call on him, Merlin knows of your intentions. He knows who you are, what situation you're requesting help with, and the best solution. But he waits before approaching you, first scanning you to see if you're a student who's willing to learn over the long haul—or if you're someone who just wants a quick fix.

Merlin comes to those who have a sincere desire to learn the spiritual secrets of alchemy, Divine magic, and manifestation skills that will be used in the light and not for personal glorification. He emphasizes to his students that these skills must never be used to harm or destroy anyone or anything physically or emotionally. Merlin's knowledge is his prized possession, and he shares it willingly with those whose hearts are loving and pure.

It doesn't hurt to call upon Merlin even if you're not sure that you're ready. *He* knows. Simply think his name and mentally ask him to come and assist you. If you're ready to learn and work, you will feel his presence and mentally hear his words. If you're not ready, Merlin will guide you to an archangel or master who can prepare you for readiness. Either way, thank Merlin for his loving care.

Moses
(Judeo-Christian)

The Prophet Moses was called upon by God to lead his people out of slavery in Egypt and to the "promised land of milk and honey" in Israel. He and the 12 tribes of Israel wandered through the desert and across the vast lands. Finally, after 40 years of constant travel, Moses was compelled to climb Mount Sinai, where he received an assurance from God that his people would be led to their promised land. Moses received Commandments from God that he was asked to deliver to the Israelites. These Commandments formed the basis for monotheism—the First Commandment being not to worship any other gods.

Moses was born in 15th-century B.C. Egypt to Amram and Jochebed. The Pharoah, who was threatened by the increasing power and wealth of the Jewish people, ordered the murder of all newborn Jewish babies. Moses' mother placed her baby in a waterproof reed basket and set him to float down the Nile river, where she hoped he would attract the attention and compassion of the Pharoah's daughter. Her plan worked, and Moses was raised in the palace of the Pharaoh as if he were born of royalty.

Biblical accounts that tell of God teaching Moses to perform miraculous feats include: Moses striking a rock that gave forth enough water to quench the thirst of an entire congregation and their animals; parting the Red Sea and walking through it; having clear conversations with God through a burning bush; making a serpent turn into a rod; and others. He was a testament to the miracle of faithfully following Divine guidance.

Moses helps spiritual aspirants and teachers of all faiths and religions, and he's one of my own guides. While I was sitting on New Zealand's western coastline, Moses gave me a profoundly stirring message. His words continue to help and intrigue me: *"Striving inherently places the intention forward into the future, with your focus and intent being centered on subsequent gains and improvement. So much better to stay with your current situation and attain enjoyment, and extract the sum of lessons gained from that scenario before moving on to a new game plan. Withdraw your future plans, and concentrate instead upon this moment. Notice where you are, how you arrived there, and the circumstances that led to your arrival.*

"Once an understanding has been met, turn to the next moment, and so forth. Future-tense focus keeps you trapped in a vacuum that obliterates your ability to draw nurturing, lessons, guidance, and sustenance from the present. The monumental lessons for all mortals is to learn an appreciation for whatever circumstances arise. Do not seek to switch to a new situation until you have fully extracted every minute enjoyment out of your present one. Life is about what's happening to you presently—that's all that matters."

Helps with:

- Authority figures, dealing and negotiating with
- Clear communication with God
- Courage
- Faith
- Leadership
- Miracle-working

Invocation

Moses' life story is a testament to accepting a leadership role, even if you feel unsure or unqualified to perform that function. In the same way, Moses can help you "step up to the plate" and do the best job possible. Anytime that you feel uncertain about your power or abilities, call upon Moses:

> "Beloved Moses, please lend me your courage, and help me overcome fear and cast out doubt. I ask you to fill my heart with faith in my God-given abilities. Please guide my words and actions so that I may lead and guide others according to God's will. Thank you."

Nemetona
(England)

Also known as *She of the Sacred Grove*.

Nemetona is the Celtic goddess of power places, sacred grounds and circles, labyrinths, and medicine wheels.

A shrine to Nemetona stands at the ancient healing spa, Bath, in southern England. In ancient times, Celts never held sacred ceremonies indoors—they were always held in open-air settings. Nemetona watched over these gatherings in the way that an angel or master would watch over a church or temple today.

I spoke with Nemetona, appropriately, at the sacred circle Stonehenge, not far from Bath. She struck me as being somber, stately, and stern in the most loving but no-nonsense way. Infused with ancient energy, she stands guard over power places, holding in the energy of the prayers invoked by people who visit these lands. Nemetona has overseen outdoor sacred rituals and ceremonies throughout time (she explained that they all occur simultaneously, instead of in linear time).

Nemetona said, *"When you pray in a sacred power place, you join in a simultaneous reality with ancient rituals being currently performed in a parallel dimension. Prayers for increased power, psychic abilities, and manifesting abilities join with ancient tribal dances and sacred-rite prayers."*

Helps with:

- Infusing ceremonies with guidance, overseeing wisdom, and protection
- Space clearing in your home's back and front yard

INVOCATION

When you begin a ceremony, especially one that involves having people stand or sit in a circle, or one where people walk a labyrinth, invoke Nemetona to oversee the process:

"Sacred goddess, Nemetona, we invite your presence and participation into our circle. Please infuse it with your magically loving energy, and bless all involved with our ceremony. Nemetona, please clear the space in, around, below, and above our circle. Thank you."

Oonagh
(Ireland)

Also known as *Onaugh, Oona.*

Oonagh was married to Fionnbharr, the head of the Tuatha Dé Danaans, the inhabitants of Ireland before the Gaelics took over the land. The Tuathas became leprechauns after the invasion. Oonagh was faithful and patient with her husband even though he had many affairs with human women.

In artwork, Oonagh is portrayed as having golden hair that's long enough to touch the ground. She's a goddess of devotion in love relationships, aesthetics, and magic; and she's also a fairy queen.

I called on Oonagh while sitting in the midst of an Irish fairy garden, and I saw the most beautiful vision of opalescent, shimmering, glittering light with the brightest fairy in the middle, glowing from the inside. I could hear music like a celestial choir, and instrumental hums emanating from her, as if her every move elicited an electric rhapsody of melodies. Oonagh didn't say anything—she just beamed with joy, love, and beauty.

When I asked Oonagh what she wanted to tell the readers of this book, she simply gushed, *"Love."* After a few moments of pregnant silence, she continued: *"Be in Love. Not 'in love,' as in relationship love with just one other person, but be stationed in the midst of Love. That is what you see glowing around me. That is why your breath deepened, you smiled, and your heart rate increased when you first caught sight of me.*

"It is I who inspires ballet and other lovely dance, for the flower fairies

have taught us all to be graceful ballerina dancers in so many ways. Use movement to make your heart swell with excitement and gratitude. Being stationary too long makes your legs swell and your body feel old and tired. Call upon me for the motivation to exercise, and I shall visit you at twilight and again just before dawn. I shall sprinkle over you my magical and potent fairy dust to get you moving upon awakening. I shall act as a physical therapist and dance coach to encourage you to stretch, sway, dance to rhythms in nature and music, and enjoy the beauty and grace of your heavenly body. Live in love."

Helps with:

- Beauty and attractiveness
- Dance and movement
- Divine magic
- Exercise and motivation
- Fairies, contacting
- Love relationships, all aspects of

INVOCATION

Oonagh loves to dance and move her body, and she loves it when we engage in this activity with her. To synchronize yourself to Oonagh's presence, imagine yourself as a graceful ballerina (male or female), dancing among the flowers. Better yet, stand up and dance in an imagined or real field of flowers. As you move around (in your imagination or in reality), think the word *love* repeatedly. Then, mentally ask Oonagh to dance with you. As she moves alongside you, have a mental conversation with her about your love life. Hold nothing back—tell her everything that's on your mind: your worries, desires, past relationship issues, and current situations. Notice how she lifts heaviness out of your heart during this conversation and helps you to feel light and carefree, which is the essence of faith. Thank Oonagh for her dance and her assistance.

Pele

(Hawaii)

Also known as *Ka-'ula-o-ke-ahi: Redness of the Fire.*

Pele is the fire goddess who rules Hawaii's volcanos and takes various forms: a young, beautiful woman; a wizened crone; a dog; and a flame. In the Hawaiian islands, Pele is highly respected as a powerful deity.

Many legends surround Pele's origination. A common theme is Pele's sibling rivalry with her older sister, Hiiaka, goddess of the ocean. When Pele decided to use her firepower to bring land up from the sea to create new islands, her sister battled her. Hiiaka poured water onto Pele's beloved lava, and steam from the two warring sisters poured out of the volcanos.

Other tales are of Pele's tragic love affairs with mortals and gods. The lava is said to be Pele's hair and tears from her anguish over her love life. It's been said that taking lava rocks from the Hawaiian islands will result in Pele's wrath. Supposedly, many tourists have mailed back lava to the islands to undo bad-luck streaks that occurred after bringing the lava home.

Pele is a powerful yet trustworthy goddess who helps us tap in to our passions and true heart's desires. In Kona, she told me, *"We each have burning fire within us, fire that when properly channeled, fuels us with passion and a sense of purpose. If we deny ourselves as we follow our desires and passions, we may erupt in a volcano of fury. Even then, however, we can turn our anger and indignation into creative forms of beauty, much like when my lava flow hardens and turns to rock, allowing new soil and extensions of my islands to be formed."*

Pele also helps us be more honest in relationships, especially when we're feeling angry or hurt. She knows that if we keep our feelings buried within us, the hidden anger will smother and extinguish the flames of passion, or else explode like a volcano. Ask her for guidance when you need to tell someone that you're angry with them so that you can keep the passion in that relationship alive.

Helps with:

- Empowerment
- Energy
- Goal-setting and goal-getting
- Honest communication in relationships
- Passion
- Prioritizing

INVOCATION

As the goddess of sacred fire, Pele helps us burn a flame of passion in our careers, relationships, and lives as a whole. If you feel that your life is colorless in any way, call upon Pele for help. First, light a warm-colored candle (such as red, orange, yellow, or white), then stare at the flame and say with great reverence and respect:

"Sacred goddess Pele, I ask for your help in reigniting my inner flame. Help me be illuminated with passion for life. [If you have a special project or relationship that you'd like to get enthusiastic about, describe it to her now.] Help me temper this passion with loving kindness, and summon up the courage to speak my truth if anger arises within me."

Saint Francis
(Catholic)

Also known as *Saint Francis of Assisi, Francis Bernardone, Poverello.*

Born Francis Bernardone in 1181, in Assisi, Italy, into a rich family, Francis spent his youth getting into his share of trouble. As a young adult, he served part time as a soldier, during which time he was imprisoned. It was in that Perugia jail that Francis had a epiphany, wherein he heard Jesus tell him to put aside his worldly life. This experience profoundly changed him, and when he was released, he followed a path of spirituality and devotion.

Francis led the life of an acetic, dressing and acting like a beggar while preaching about Jesus and peace. He volunteered in hospitals, ministering to the sick, and formed a spiritual order called The Franciscans in 1212.

Francis may be best remembered for his Dr. Doolittle-like interactions with animals. Legend says that during an outing, he saw a flock of birds. As Francis stopped and began preaching to them, the birds cocked their heads and behaved like members of an enthralled audience. After Francis was done, he walked next to the birds, even brushing them with his jacket, and they didn't move. After that experience, Francis began preaching to birds, animals, and reptiles about God's love. They responded to him as tame, rather than wild, animals. For instance, the birds would become quiet as he spoke, and a wild rabbit continually jumped on his lap even after he put it on the ground several times. Similarly, a wolf accused of killing and harming both people and animals became placid under Francis's loving guidance.

He wrote many prayers and meditations, including the famous Prayer of Saint Francis:

Lord, make me an instrument of your peace;
where there is hatred, let me sow love;
when there is injury, pardon;
where there is doubt, faith;
where there is despair, hope;
where there is darkness, light;
and where there is sadness, joy.
O Divine Master, grant that I may not so
much seek to be consoled as to console;
to be understood, as to understand,
to be loved as to love;
for it is in giving that we receive,
it is in pardoning that we're pardoned,
and it's in dying [to ourselves] *that we're born to eternal life.*

Francis passed into the spirit world on October 4, 1226, and two years later, he was canonized as Saint Francis of Assisi.

I've seen Saint Francis in the presence of many of my clients who are animal lovers, or whose life purpose involves helping and healing these wonderful creatures. He continues to be a passionate advocate of animals, and helps us learn from these wise and gentle beings with whom we share the planet.

Helps with:

- Animal communication and healing
- Career, finding a meaningful
- Environmentalism

- Life's purpose, finding one's
- Peace, personal and global
- Spiritual devotion
- Youths trying to overcome delinquency

INVOCATION

Since Saint Francis is so closely associated with nature and animals, you'll feel the greatest connection with him in a natural setting or when you're with your pets or other animals. A kind, grandfatherly being, Saint Francis will come to anyone who calls upon him, especially if you're willing to help animals or the environment. If you're outside in nature, use all of your senses to enjoy the beauty: smell the fragrances, listen to the sounds, and feel the wind blowing past you. If you're indoors with pets, use your senses to notice details as well. The point is to slow down and appreciate nature's intricacies and loveliness.

As you're immersed in appreciation, mentally ask Saint Francis to join you (chances are that he already has before you even called upon him). When you sense his presence, take a few moments to talk to him cordially, just like you're engaging in conversation with a friend.

Saint Francis always asks us to take our time and appreciate the moment, so you needn't rush while asking Saint Francis for help or for a Divine assignment. Just enjoy the mental conversation, and allow the topics to naturally flow to the point where you request his assistance. As you develop this bond of friendship, you'll start to mutually support one another—you from your vantage point on the Earth plane, and he from his heavenly home.

Saint-Germain
(New Age)

Also known as *Comte de Saint-Germain, The Count of Saint-Germain, der Wundermann, Saint Germaine, Saint Germain, The Wonderman of Europe.*

Saint-Germain isn't a saint in the Catholic sense and shouldn't be confused with "Saint Germaine Cousin" or "Saint Germanus," two actual Catholic saints. Instead, he was a real man who was a royal count of the French region called "Saint-Germain."

His real full name is Comte de Saint-Germain, or The Count of Saint-Germain. He was a man born of royal blood somewhere between 1690 and 1710, although reports conflict as to his parents' lineage. Some say that his mother was Marie de Neubourg, the widow of King Charles II of Spain, and that his father was Comte Adanero. Others (particularly those associated with Theosophy) hold that his father was Prince Ragoczy of Transylvania. A few reports say that *he* was Prince Ragoczy. Still others claim that he's a Portugese Jew.

Regardless of his origin, history shows that Count Saint-Germain rubbed elbows with high society and European royalty. He was multi-talented, playing the violin like a virtuoso, giving psychic readings, mastering numerous languages, and painting exquisite artwork. He also spent time studying and teaching occult and alchemy subjects, and he was involved with the founding of several secret societies, including the

Freemasons. He boasted of being able to turn lead into gold, and to know of a secret technique to remove flaws from diamonds while increasing their size.

In addition, Saint-Germain gave his friends elixirs that would supposedly erase wrinkles and restore youth. This might be true, as most reports of note say that he looked like a youthful middle-aged man throughout his life. It's also said that, although he frequently dined out with friends, he never ate in public. He told many people that the only food he ever ate was a special oatmeal concoction that he made at home.

Reports say that Saint-Germain was quite wealthy, although no source of his wealth was ever established. He was enamored with gemstones—or were they crystals?—and he carried them with him, often giving them as gifts. He painted gems in his artwork in strong, bold colors.

Saint-Germain kept details about his birth and personal history private, and he was considered a fascinatingly mysterious man in his day. Occasionally he'd make references to past lives—for example, saying that he was with Nero in Rome. He also remarked that he'd return to France in 100 years. Prince Charles of Hesse-Kassel, whom Saint-Germain lived and practiced alchemy with, reported that the count died at his castle on February 27, 1784. However, many credible accounts show that Saint-Germain was seen several years later. For instance, official Freemason documents reportedly show that Saint-Germain was the French representative at their 1785 convention.

Saint-Germain was also deeply involved in French politics and worked alongside King Louis XVI on several missions. It's believed that he (Saint-Germain) was partially responsible for Catherine the Great taking the throne.

A visionary who offered his psychic visions freely, Saint-Germain gave private readings to royalty and those of social influence. For example, he told Marie Antoinette of his prophecies about the French Revolution 15 years before it occurred. Occasionally Saint-Germain's behavior and eccentricities got him into trouble, and he was arrested at least once.

Some people believe that Saint-Germain attained immortality, and that he faked his death to avoid attracting undue attention. Annie Besant, one of the original Theosophists, claimed to have met him in

1896. Guy Ballard, whose pen name is Godre Ray King, wrote about meeting Saint-Germain at Mount Shasta, California, in the 1930s. Recently, Elizabeth Clare Prophet wrote and lectured about Saint-Germain, emphasizing her belief that he carries a violet flame to transmute lower energies.

The "I AM Teachings," a New Age work related to the Great White Brotherhood [see Glossary] considers Saint-Germain's role in history highly important. In New Age circles, it's believed that his past lives include Joseph, father of Jesus; Merlin; Shakespeare; and Christopher Columbus. He's regarded as being the Lord or Chohan of the Seventh Ray, which is the high-frequency violet color in the hierarchy of color vibrations. In other words, he's a very important figure in the ascension movement for the human race and the Great White Brotherhood.

My first remarkable experience with Saint-Germain happened while teaching a beginning psychic-development class in Atlanta. Students were paired up, facing each other, giving each other readings. When the students were done, I asked them to share their experiences with me. A woman in one corner of the room raised her hand. She was a Jewish woman who was new to New Age teachings. Her partner during the reading was a Catholic priest from England who'd flown to Atlanta to take my class.

"Who is Saint-Germain?" the woman asked me. Neither she nor her partner had ever heard of this man who'd come through their reading so strongly.

"I got Saint-Germain, too!" said another student in the opposite corner of the room. "Me, too!" exclaimed two other students. What was remarkable was that the four students who'd encountered Saint-Germain during the reading had never even heard of him before, and they'd been sitting in different corners of the room. Saint-Germain was showing us that he was there, and that he was all around us. I understood that day that he would be co-instructing my students.

I've come to know Saint-Germain as a loving, benevolent ascended master who wishes to work with lightworkers—that is, people who want to help the world clean up its act. He provides guidance, protection, and courage. If those sound like qualities that Archangel Michael provides, it's no accident, since the two work hand-in-wing together.

Helps with:

- Alchemy
- Authority figures and influential people, comfortably interacting with
- Courage
- Direction
- Life purpose
- Miraculous manifestations
- Perseverance
- Psychic protection
- Space clearing

INVOCATION

In my experience, people don't call Saint-Germain—he's the one who calls first! He seems to just show up wherever lightworkers are gathered in classes, study groups, or prayer meetings. He works with spiritual teachers to encourage their outgoing nature and leadership skills.

That's not to say, however, that you can't request a special audience with him when you desire a message or some type of motivation. Simply think, *Saint-Germain, I need your help.* Wait a moment, and then mentally let him know the situation or question with which you need assistance.

You'll know that he's with you because a creative answer will come to you suddenly. You may also see violet-purple sparkles of light in the room. Or, you may start seeing violet-purple everywhere you go, on people's clothing or on flowers, for instance. You'll also begin thinking or writing profound thoughts on how to help others.

Saint John of God

(Catholic)

Also known as *João Cidade, Juan Ciudad, Father of the Poor.*

Saint John of God is the patron of the mentally and physically ill and hospital employees, and he also helps booksellers and those with heart ailments.

He was born João (which means "John" in English) Cidade, in Portugal in 1495. At age eight, he and his family moved to Spain. As a young man, he worked as a shepherd, a soldier, and a traveling book peddler. In 1538, he had an epiphany after hearing John of Avila speak on repentance. João gave away his money and belongings and was subsequently hospitalized in a psychiatric wing of the Royal Hospital.

In his opinion, the hospitalization experience was degrading and dreadful, and he decided to devote his life to upgrading hospital treatment. After his release from the hospital, he was homeless and disillusioned, which helped him develop a very strong affinity with other homeless and disenfranchised people.

João worked tirelessly to reach many people who suffered from illness (mental and physical) and deprivations of all types. In the beginning, when the weather was inclement, he would share the porch of a friend's house with those needing shelter. This began The Hospitaller Order of Saint John of God, which today, 450 years after it was founded, continues to provide shelter to people throughout the world.

He also bought a facility and cared for poor, homeless, sick, and unwanted people in his new hometown of Granada, Spain. João was known to give what he could, beg for those who couldn't, and even help carry those who could not walk. His motto was: *"Labor without stopping. Do all the good works you can while you still have the time,"* and he was known to counsel others by citing the Biblical verse: *"Whatever you do to one of the least of these, my brothers and sisters, you do to me."*

When someone was admitted to his hospital, legend says that he or his staff would wash the person, feed them, and then pray with them. Empathetic and encouraging, he listened to everyone's problems and offered his most sincere advice. People were so impressed by his dedication and honesty that they gave him money and volunteered to help him in his ministry. It was these people who gave him the title "John of God."

Using his position with the powerful, he advocated successfully for the poor to improve their condition. Due to contributions and the work of dedicated volunteers, John of God's mission continues to spread the message and the practice of "hospitality." John died of pneumonia on March 8, 1550, while immersed in prayer after saving a man who'd almost drowned.

Saint John of God is a jolly fellow who exudes joy. Just calling upon him is enough to elevate the mood and lift the spirits. He reassures those who are depressed or worried, and helps people feel physically, emotionally, and financially safe and secure. Invoke him at the first sign of sadness, or to heal a broken heart.

Helps with:

- Anxiety
- Depression
- Healing
- Heart ailments
- Hospitalizations
- Joy, increasing
- Space clearing
- Spiritual dedication

INVOCATION

Saint John of God comes to anyone of any religious or spiritual faith who calls upon him, just by thinking of his name. You can also ask him to visit your loved ones or clients who are depressed or anxious. Or, you can hold this prayer in mind to call him to your side:

"Golden-hearted Saint John of God, please bring me the joy of God, which you exude. Please surround me with your loving care and attention. Help me banish pessimistic thoughts and attitudes, and rise above the appearance of problems. Help me trust in Divine order and let go of the need to control. Please help me have a mind filled with faith, a heart filled with joy, and a voice filled with laughter. Please guide me so that I may live your legacy of helping others and serving God. Amen."

Saint Padre Pio
(Catholic)

Also known as *Francesco Forgione, Padre Pio.*

Born Francesco Forgione on May 25, 1887, in Naples, Italy, Francesco changed his name to Pio, which means "Pius," when he entered the Capuchin monastery at age 16. Padre Pio began experiencing the *stigmata*—a condition characterized by pain, open wounds, or blood appearing in the same places on the body where Jesus was impaled with nails and a thorny crown. The stigmata wounds and blood remained visible for the next 50 years.

Many have verified miraculous healings associated with Padre Pio, both during his mortal life and beyond. He's renowned for helping the blind to see and healing various injuries and seemingly incurable ailments. During his life, Padre Pio was able to bilocate, levitate, and accurately predict the future. He also founded a hospital and a series of prayer groups.

Saint Padre Pio is a very spirited divinity with a lot of enthusiasm, joy, and a persona that reveals his deep faith and optimism. He has an infectious and optimistic outlook, and just by calling him, you're likely to feel uplifted.

Helps with:

- Eyesight, including blindness
- Forgiveness
- Healers, increasing the abilities of
- Healing of all kinds
- Prophecy
- Spiritual growth

INVOCATION

During his life, Padre Pio performed many healings from his confessional booth. He asked people to admit the true underlying source of their pain aloud. You can do the same while calling upon Padre Pio for intercession. He helps people of all religions and creeds equally. An example of an invocation might be:

"Beloved Saint Padre Pio, please help me to [describe the situation]. I admit that this problem has stirred up disturbing feelings such as [name whatever emotions you can]. I'm willing to completely forgive myself and the others in this situation, and I ask that you help me do so. Please help me reveal light, love, and forgiveness. Thank you, God. Thank you, Jesus. Thank you, Saint Padre Pio. Amen."

Saint Therese
(Catholic)

Also known as *Therese of Lisieux, Therese of the Child Jesus,*
The Little Flower, The Little Flower of Jesus.

Saint Therese is a powerful and loving healing saint from France.
You'll know that she's heard your prayers when you see or smell
roses. She was born Therese Martin in 1873, and at age 15 became a
nun at a Carmelite convent. At the young age of 24, she passed away.

Many people report verified healings after praying to Saint Therese
or visiting her relics. As Therese lay dying in 1897, she said, "After my
death, I will let fall a shower of roses." Since that time, she's been associated with those beautiful flowers. For that reason, she's the patron saint
of florists; however, she helps with so much more, particularly in the
area of physical healing.

It's been said that she helped many aviators during World War II, so
she's also considered a patron saint of pilots, flight attendants, and air-
based military personnel.

In her autobiography, *The Story of a Soul,* Therese discussed how
simplicity, and also trusting and loving God, were the keys to living a
happy and sacred life. She said that what matters in life "is not great
deeds, but great love."

I first met Saint Therese when I was meditating in 1994. I loved
meditating so much that I'd spend hours sitting with my eyes shut, just

listening and enjoying the wonderful feelings of peace and Divine love. One day I heard a woman's voice talking to me. She said, *"Little Flower,"* then she said, *"Saint Therese."* Not having a Catholic background, I didn't know who she was, so I called a local Catholic church and asked the priest for information. He patiently explained Saint Therese's background to me, and told me about her connection to Little Flower.

The priest was so kind that I summoned up the courage to tell him about my experience during meditation. He was very open-minded and accepting, and told me that he thought Saint Therese was with me because of my work as a spiritual counselor and healer. He explained that she helps sincere people, regardless of faith.

Since that time, I've seen Saint Therese with other people to whom I've given readings. Sometimes she's with women who are named Therese or Theresa. It's wonderful to know that I still have her as a constant and steady companion and guide as well.

Helps with:

- Gardening—especially flowers
- Healing all forms of illness or injury
- Pilots and airline crews
- Spiritual counseling

INVOCATION

Catholics normally recite the Novena Rose Prayer to ask for Saint Therese's blessings. Non-Catholics may also request this loving saint's assistance. It's said that if you practice this devotion for 9 to 24 days, you'll see a rose as a sign that your request has been heard and granted:

"O Little Therese of the Child Jesus, please pick for me
a rose from the heavenly gardens and send it to me as a
message of love. O Little Flower of Jesus, ask God today to
grant the favors I now place with confidence in your hands
[mention specific requests]. Saint Therese, help me to always
believe as you did in God's great love for me so that I might
imitate your 'Little Way' each day. Amen."

Sanat Kumara
(Hindu; Vedic; New Age)

◖✦◗

Also known as *Karttikeya, Sumara, Skanda-Karttikeya.*

Kumara is a warrior god, devoted to ridding people and the earth of negative entities and lower energies.

Legends abound explaining Kumara's creation, with the common thread being his relationship to the number six—perhaps because of his talents in banishing negative spirits. One tale recounts that Heaven was plagued with demons, so Shiva used his third-eye flame to beget six children who would specialize in slaying demons. However, their mother hugged the six children with such enthusiastic love that she squeezed their bodies into one child with six heads.

Hindus revere Kumara as a leader among gods who banishes darkness in the minds of men and spirits. His demon-slaying activities are thought to be metaphorical, symbolizing Kumara's slaying of ignorance.

In New Age circles, he's hailed as a member of the Great White Brotherhood, working alongside Jesus and Archangel Michael to help the planet and her population with the ascension process.

Sanat Kumara says, *"Power is my focus—power for one and for all . . . redelivering personal power to people everywhere, direct from the Great Source of All. Through my realization of the Great Allness, I am able to tap in to its plentitude and draw up from the power supply and distribute it to everyone. By illuminating the masses with this personal power, there's an infusion of justice and grace in the world, for no one can usurp your personal boundaries when you know that your supply of power is unlimited and completely unfettered. Lean on this knowledge, and never be afraid to exercise your rights in all situations that call upon you to be strong."*

Helps with:

- Ego, overcoming
- Fatigue, lifting
- Healing work
- Space clearing
- Spirit releasement
- Spiritual knowledge and enlightenment

INVOCATION

Kumara is a powerful spirit who has a primal, indigenous feel to him, like an intense witch doctor. When you call upon him, Kumara responds at lightning speed and with lovingly powerful energy. If you're fatigued, call upon him for help:

"Sanat Kumara, please bring me your powerful energy to uplift my spirit and vitality. Please help me rise above negative thoughts and emotions, like a bird above dark clouds. I ask your assistance in tapping me in to the true and eternal Source of all energy. Please clear away lower spirits and energies from within and around me, and infuse me with Divine healing light."

Then breathe deeply while Kumara does his work. In a few moments, you should feel revived and refreshed.

Sedna
(Inuit/Eskimo)

Also known as *Ai-willi-ay-o, Nerivik.*

Various legends say that Sedna fell (or was thrown) off her parents' boat, and that dismembered parts of her body formed the sea lions and other sea creatures. Sedna is considered the Creator goddess of all inhabitants of the sea—the *ultimate* sea goddess.

Sedna will grant wishes to those who go to the sea—and who ask her lovingly, honestly, and gently for favors. Since she's so connected with water and dolphins, Sedna also helps with intuition and brings messages about dolphins into one's dreamtime.

I invoked Sedna while sitting on a boat in the middle of the Pacific ocean near Hawaii. Although she's available for help and guidance anywhere, I wanted to meet Sedna at her home to ask her for a message for this book. She began by saying, *"I'm the mistress of the great ocean, which brings magic to your atmosphere. Weather arises from the ocean currents, moisture, and winds.*

"Caution is warranted regarding the care and protection of this massive water surface. Aside from not discarding your waste products into the sea, your incessant use of cleaning supplies must, must, must be averted—this very minute!

"Water itself is enough to engender cleanliness—it's purity, inherent blessings, and life-giving qualities can be used instead of soapsuds to wash

away grime. Hot water will remove germs in and of itself—no need for disinfectants, which are polluting the waters and atmosphere of this last remaining great planet.

"Allow me to help replace your cares and worries with magical underwater adventures that I can channel to you during your dreamtime. Call upon me for wishes whenever you like, and cast your cares and worries to me now. I will swallow them into my cavernous sea and wash them until the underlying essence of your concerns is revealed . . . and then healed. Take good care of my darlings—the sea lions, dolphins, and fish—for me."

Helps with:

- Abundance—especially food supply
- Animal rights—especially relating to water-based animals, fish, and birds
- Dolphins and whales
- Dreams and intuition
- The granting of wishes when you're in the ocean
- Hands and fingers, healing
- Hurricanes, dispelling
- Ocean conservation
- Protection while swimming, sailing, or surfing

INVOCATION

It's best to connect with Sedna when you're in or around water, as this is her domain. Say to her:

"Dearest Sedna, Goddess of the waters, I desire to develop a connection with you through my intuition and dreamtime. Please bring me a clear message about [name the situation you'd like help with]. Please bring the dolphins into my dreams and help me uncover the truth about this situation. Thank you."

Serapis Bey
(Egypt, Greece, and New Age)

Also known as *Serapis, Apis, Asar-Apis, Osiris-Apis.*

Originally an Egyptian god of the underworld named Serapis who was in charge of the ascension at Luxor, Egypt; in New Age circles, he's now known as Serapis Bey. He helps people work toward ascension through spiritual enlightenment. Serapis Bey motivates people toward physical fitness and healthful lifestyles due to his interest in beauty and aesthetics; he also helps them withstand the coming changes that are prophesied. Like a spiritual fitness guru, he inspires, motivates, and provides hope for the future.

Serapis Bey also helps artists and musicians with their creative projects. An extremely loving ascended master, he's actively involved in averting war and bringing peace to Earth.

I've long had an affinity and affection for Serapis Bey, and have found him to be a wonderful coach who lovingly demands the best from us. He pushes us to take exceptional care of our bodies, and if you begin working with him, expect to be given some pointers on exercise and nutrition.

He says, *"Once again, we're reunited, as I've been with so many of you countless times before. You're here for another initiation, are you? Another rung on the ladder of ascension for you. I'm here to help you carefully and cautiously choose your next move. Many of you are rushing so much that you can no longer hear your inward guide. You <u>must</u> create silent space for yourself.*

"Get away from the frantic pace and worldly noise at regular intervals. Even a brief break will refresh you and reconnect you to the Voice you love with all of your heart, the Voice you trust uppermost. When you allow yourself to become distant or disconnected from this Voice, you feel insecure and afraid for reasons unknown to you. You become like an infant pulled away from her mother's nursing breast: lost and confused.

"Make the Voice your uppermost priority, a valuable friend whom you vigilantly keep track of. If you cannot hear the Voice, it's simply a sign to become quiet and still momentarily until you regain awareness of this inner source of guidance and direction."

Helps with:

- Addictions and cravings, overcoming
- Artists, musicians, and creative endeavors
- Ascension
- Clear communication with God
- Exercise and weight-loss motivation
- Peace, personal and global
- Prophecy

INVOCATION

Serapis Bey can be contacted anytime you need loving care, spiritual insight, or peace and quiet. Hold the mental intention of connecting with him, then stop a moment, close your eyes, and take some deep breaths. As you inhale, think about your desires. As you exhale, imagine that you're releasing whatever is bothering you. You'll feel or sense Serapis Bey's presence alongside you, mirroring your breathing pattern. At some point, you'll either hear his voice or sense some thoughts that come from him.

Don't worry—Serapis Bey won't override your free will. However, he *will* give you clear guidance and instructions about self-improvement, along with the motivation to undertake these endeavors. As you go through any process requiring stamina and focus, call him to your side.

Solomon
(Judeo-Christian)

Also known as *King Solomon.*

Solomon was the king of Israel, following his father, King David's, reign in the 900 B.C. era. In light of King David's intensity, Solomon was viewed as a gentle and wise man who blended alchemy and Judaic mysticism with common sense and wisdom. Solomon was instrumental in many of Israel's advances in government and architecture. Most notable is Solomon's overseeing of the construction of the Temple of God, in which the Ark of the Covenant was housed.

The book of 1 Kings in the Bible makes reference to Solomon's remarkable wisdom: *"Solomon's wisdom surpassed the wisdom of all the sons of the east and all the wisdom of Egypt. For he was wiser than all men. . . . Men came from all peoples to hear the wisdom of Solomon. . . ."*

References in the Torah, Gospels, and ancient Judaic texts refer to Solomon's exorcism and magical skills. A 15th-century Greek manuscript called *The Testament of Solomon* describes him using a magical ring (known as "Solomon's Ring") that has a Star of David engraved on top. Scholars point out that the six-pointed star was originally associated with cabalism, high magic, and Pythagorean mysticism. Solomon may have been instrumental in making it a symbol of Israel and Judaism.

The Testament of Solomon also contains one of the numerous accounts of Solomon controlling demons, both to banish them and to control them as "spiritual slaves" to perform magical duties. Texts about Solomon usually discuss him banishing and controlling 72 particular demons, each with a specific name and function. Before he left Earth, Solomon contained these 72 demons so that they wouldn't disturb people.

Solomon has ascended to such a high level that you may not feel his presence when you call upon him. Instead, your higher consciousness will tap in to his collective wisdom. He's a wise, old sage similar to the God archetype who sees all and knows all, and he already knows who you are, what your Divine assignment is, and how you can do things better and more efficiently. He'll help you improve different areas of your life, which is sometimes frightening or irritating to those who misconstrue his messages as a power or control struggle. But those who are wise will be open to his assistance.

Solomon says, *"Poetry is the name of life. Poetry is artistry in motion. For it's not the accumulation of knowledge to which we're aspiring, but the ability to live life in a grander, more fluid, and more aristocratic fashion. To take charge through godliness of your inner demons and squeeze out all excess so that you may truly reign with princely power over your domain. Get control of all your faculties. Handle addictions and patterns directly, and be free—free to rule, free to live, and free to express your inward callings in boundless ways."*

Helps with:

- Cabalistic understanding
- Divine magic
- Joy
- Manifestation
- Space clearing
- Spirit releasement
- Wisdom and understanding

INVOCATION

Call upon Solomon to help you with any difficult or seemingly impossible situation. As a Divine magician, he'll direct sacred energy to support you:

"Solomon, O Solomon, I need your help and assistance, please, and I need it now. Please come to me and shine light on this situation [describe it to him], and help loosen the chains of fear and unforgiveness. I need a miracle, and I need it now. Help resolve this matter, and lift me out of the trenches of darkness. Thank you for your wisdom and courage, and for providing the perfect solution to this matter."

Sulis
(British)

Also known as *Sul, Sulla, Sulevia, Sulivia.*

An ancient goddess of healing waters whose shrine was at the Bath spa in southern England, Sulis's name means "eye" and "seeing." So it makes sense that she helps with physical and psychic vision. The eye is also associated with the sun, so Sulis is known as a sun goddess, which is rare, as male deities are usually sun gods, while female deities have moon and star connections. This solar association may stem from Sulis's relationship with hot springs.

Sulis oversees all pools of water associated with healing, especially natural hot springs. Today in Bath, people come from all over the world to drink from her well in the center of the hot spring's restaurant. The water is rich with sulphur, and is said to function as a fountain of youth.

I spoke with Sulis near Bath, and she said: *"It was I whom you saw in the rainbow over Stonehenge. I'm in the prism effect of water drops, reflecting the Divine light inherent in all water, including oxygen. Plants are precious to me, and yes, as you asked, I can help gardeners grow everything from bumper crops to healthy houseplants. Just don't expect me to rid plants of aphids—I'm a natural horticulturist who respects the balance between the Earth kingdom (which the insects truly reign over—think of their hardiness as a testament to their regalness) and the plant community."*

Helps with:

- Blessings
- Clairvoyance
- Eyesight, physical and spiritual
- Gardening
- Water used in ceremonies
- Wishes

INVOCATION

It's a good idea to invite Sulis to any ceremony involving water. You can conduct a version of a water ceremony by drawing a hot bath and filling it with sea salt, essential oils, and a few flower petals. Surround the bathtub with candles, soft music, and at least one potted plant. Dim the lights, ignite the candles, and as you get in the bathtub, say:

"Sister Sulis, I invite your loving presence. Sulis, please bring your beloved blessings, your caring nature, your spiritual vision, and your youthful beauty; and bestow it upon the waters within and around me. Please help fulfill my wish, which is [describe your wish]. Thank you, beloved Sulis. Thank you."

Tara
(Buddhist, Hindu, Jainist, Lamaist)

Also known as *Green Tara, White Tara.*

When Avalokitesvara, the *bodhisattva* (enlightened one) of compassion and protection, shed tears that formed a lake, a lotus flower rose to the top of the water. When the flower opened, a beautiful goddess stepped out of the middle, and her name was Tara. She's the female counterpart and consort of Avalokitesvara. Tara has many different sides and personalities to her, represented by different-colored Taras (Green Tara, White Tara, Red Tara, Blue Tara, and Yellow Tara). In her Yellow, Blue, and Red personas, Tara is temperamental, but as White and Green Tara, she's loving and very helpful.

Tara's name means "star," and like stars that provide navigation for sailors and travelers, Tara helps us travel smoothly and safely and find our way—whether on a trip, on our spiritual path, or just during daily life.

Green Tara is known as a "speedy" goddess who rapidly induces insight and who quickly comes to your aid. If you need emergency help physically or spiritually, call upon Green Tara.

White Tara helps increase life expectancy, and if you call upon her, she will bring you longevity. She also is a bringer of Enlightenment.

Green Tara is very intense, yet she's a very loving warrior spirit. Green Tara is a no-nonsense divinity who conducts rapid energy exchanges to help and assist those who call upon her. She says, *"I get matters settled quickly and go right to work using wisdom and action. I set my sights on an intended outcome, and bring those preferences into experience."* She attains her goals, in other words.

In contrast, White Tara is gentle, peaceful, patient, doting, nurturing, and maternal. She is the essence of purity. She approaches problems with prayer and by holding a steady focus on the beauty of Divine love. Her eyes overflow with gratitude, joy, and love. She feels and sees only love, so that's what comes forth in her presence. She says, *"I am here to shift people's hearts away from an inclination of worry. I love and I am happy, and this has a settling effect upon people whose lives I touch. It is my pleasure to spread joy far and wide."*

Both Green Tara and White Tara Help with:

- Compassion
- Protection
- Removing and avoiding obstacles

Green Tara helps with:

- Emergency aid
- Overcoming fear
- Understanding and insight

White Tara helps with:

- Enlightenment
- Longevity

INVOCATION

Green Tara: Sit quietly and meditate upon the color green while chanting *Om Tare, Tuttare Ture Svaha,* which means:

> "Tara, Swift Saviouress, please liberate me from all forms of suffering and imprisonment, and help me be balanced in my spirituality."

White Tara: Sit quietly, breathe deeply, and meditate upon the color sky blue. Then pray to White Tara:

> "Please let me be like you, White Tara, filled with compassion and grace. I am you, White Tara. I am Tara. I am Tara."

Feel yourself filled with overflowing warm love, joy, and compassion.

Thoth
(Egypt)

Also known as *Aah, Aah Tehuti, Djehuti, Tehuti, Thout, Zehuti.*

The Egyptian god of high magic, manifestation, symbols, geometry, writing, music, and astronomy, Thoth was the scribe of the gods, and he penned many books about Hermetic secrets of magic and manifestation. Legend says that one of his books, *The Emerald Tablets,* was written when Thoth was a priest-king in Atlantis. Thoth and the book survived Atlantis's demise, and he founded an Egyptian colony based on Atlantean wisdom.

It's said that Thoth's symbols are the basis for modern Freemasonry, and that he designed many Egyptian pyramids and temples.

Thoth was believed to materialize and heal with the use of chants, toning, and sound, along with sacred geometry, symbolism, and arithmetic. He taught the moon goddess, Isis, how to practice high magic, and he's credited with being the inventor of writing in ancient Egypt.

He says, *"You speak of Atlantis as being a peak of human knowledge, yet there are far greater cultures than these that existed on this planet and beyond. I've participated in several, and I shall continue to do so for service, sport, and adventure. The human 'race' is fast drawing to its finish line, and it's time for all of us to withdraw and go home. This is the natural cycle and evolution of every great culture—to reach its peak and then withdraw, like seasons of life itself. Expansion, withdrawal, expansion, withdrawal. Do not fear either route, for your [he meant everyone's] safe passage is assured. You will be applauded for your participation, which takes courage and bravery indeed.*

"*My words are not to alert you to mass destruction, but to thrust upon you an imperative: Your technology must shift to becoming air-based instead of land-based. Air-based stations can withstand the impact of your electrical currents, while your land and water suffers greatly from this assignment. Move your source of electricity to satellite components before the world goes dark with overload. You're nearing capacity right now.*

"*Reduce your dependency upon technology immediately, and return to more natural conditions. This is the only peaceful way out of the experiment. Modern conveniences have made many of you fat, lazy, and slothlike. Get up and realize your potential! Attain fitness, everyone! I do not mean to chastise you, but to motivate you with my deepest honor, love, and respect.*"

Helps with:

- Divine magic
- Life purpose
- Mathematics
- Prophecy and divination
- Psychic abilities
- Sacred geometry
- Teaching
- Writing

INVOCATION

Call upon Thoth whenever you need psychic insight, or when you seek Divine magic to help resolve a situation. His name is difficult to say without feeling like you're lisping, so when you invoke Thoth, a smile may come to your face. This mirth and joy is appealing to Thoth, so don't worry about offending him. Say aloud or mentally:

"Beloved Thoth, I call your name as your student of the Divine secrets that you so lovingly teach. Thank you for your guidance and instruction in resolving [name the situation you need help with]. Please help me be open to the power so that it may run through me as a Divine channel. Thank you, teacher. Thank you, Thoth."

Vesta

(Roman; New Age)

Also known as *Hestia, Prisca.*

Vesta is a sun and fire goddess who oversees the home and hearth. In ancient times, a sacred fire was continuously burned and tended in her honor by vestal virgins. Every fire was thought to contain part of Vesta's living spirit.

In New Age circles, Vesta works with Helios, the Roman sun god, as Solar Logos. This term denotes divinities who light the flame of the light-body within spiritual aspirants, using the sun rays from one's solar plexus.

Vesta showed me an image of herself on a chariot with Apollo, riding among the heavenly stars each evening, and tucking in those of us on Earth each night. Blessing and protecting us, I saw her showering each of us with compassion, as she recognizes the tough job we all have to do. She's similar to Archangel Haniel, who illuminates us with stardust so that we'll remember our magical properties and qualities.

Helps with:

- Divine light—increasing its size, brightness, and visibility
- Fire control
- Home—filling it with warmth and love

- Passion, igniting and keeping
- Protection—especially for children
- Space clearing

INVOCATION

It's a good idea to invite Vesta into your home if there's been recent friction among those who live there. Vesta can clear the energy of fear and anger so that future conflict is less likely to occur. She'll bring a feeling of warmth, love, and ease to the household, which will comfort all who enter the home.

Since Vesta is the goddess of the hearth or fireplace, one way to call her is by lighting a fire or a candle. As you light the flame, say to her:

"Beloved Vesta, please bring your flame of Divine love into this household and light the fire of kindness, compassion, and understanding within everyone who lives and visits this home. Help us to burn away any fears concerning love, and to feel warm and secure."

Vywamus
(New Age)

Vywamus is an ascended spiritual teacher and healer who helps lightworkers awaken their inner power and spiritual gifts, and discover their life's purpose. New Age teachers say that Vywamus is a holographic higher-self aspect of Sanat Kumara. In this respect, Vywamus and Sanat Kumara function as two separate individuals even though they're aspects of the same person (and in truth, we're all *one* anyway).

A very loving and compassionate guide, Vywamus assists rapidly in all aspects of emotional, mental, physical, and spiritual healing. He helps lightworkers face their shadows as a way of illuminating them with light.

A friend of mine named Morgan Ki'ilehua has had extensive experiences with Vywamus. She told me:

> "For many years in meditation I would see 'this man.' It didn't seem to matter whether I was meditating at home, following a guided-meditation CD, or in a meditation group at someone's home, 'this man' was always there. What I always found so interesting was that he always appeared the same way. He would be standing facing me, and he was very tall and slender. His pageboy-style shoulder-length hair was white. His long robe was blue and white. His face was clean-shaven, and he had a small, sharp nose with patient, gentle, small-set eyes. His age? Somewhere over 50 years old. There were never any words

spoken, never a feeling of any type of communication, yet there was a very strong sense of him being a very wise teacher. This continued for years. I now know that it was Vywamus.

"Several years ago, I met a woman named Saemmi Muth who told me that she was a channel for an entity called Vywamus and that her channelings had been appearing in the *Sedona Journal of Emergence* for about 15 years. I booked a private session with her, although I didn't quite know why, and I also felt skeptical.

"Nevertheless, I kept my appointment with Saemmi. During the session, Vywamus talked way above my head. I didn't understand what he was telling me about rays, dimensions, the spiritual hierarchy, and where my vibration was at the time. I just sat, listening in awe and still skeptical.

"Then I said to Vywamus, 'I do have two physical plane questions.' Vywamus said, *'You want to know about your father and your husband.'* 'Yes,' I replied. *'Your father is fine, he's in lesson* [my father had transitioned four years prior to this].*'* This was discussed briefly. Then Vywamus said, *'Your husband is fine, also; however he had an exit window and chose not to take it.'* (My husband, Alex, had had a brain seizure and a massive heart attack a few months before, and at that time, the doctors told me he wouldn't live through the night—yes, he's still here.) This part of the session was my proof, as Saemmi knew nothing about my father or details about my husband. I was a believer!

"A Vywamus Group started meeting in my home once a week. There were five or six of us. Once a week Saemmi would 'bring in' Vywamus, and the group would ask questions. We had some very powerful and enlightening evenings. Vywamus encouraged me to begin channeling.

"Much of my training was done by Vywamus through Saemmi. There was a particular session we had that was a major shift for me. Saemmi called prior to a 'training day' and told me that Vywamus wanted me to write down seven questions for our session. I could ask any question I wanted. My seven questions were ready when we met. As we sat at the table, Saemmi brought in Vywamus as usual. Vywamus asked me if I was ready for my questions. I said yes and began to read from my list. Vywamus stopped me and said, *'Channel me and get the answers.'*

"Trusting my abilities, I brought in Vywamus to speak through me, asked the questions, and got the answers. With the assistance of Vywamus, I now channel two meditation groups a week, have workshops on spirit communication and psychic development, and have completed three channeled, guided-meditation CDs. My journey with Vywamus has been fascinating, exciting, and informative. I could not imagine my life without him now. I'm in constant communication with this loving, wonderful cosmic being. Anyone who desires can channel Vywamus, as he's available to us all. Open your heart, use your Divine Intent, and simply listen."

Helps with:

- Direction
- Encouragement and inspiration
- Healing—spiritual, emotional, and physical
- Life purpose, all aspects of
- Motivation and overcoming procrastination
- Talents, discovering your

INVOCATION

As mentioned above, my friend Morgan Ki'ilehua teaches classes on connecting with Vywamus. On the next page is an invocation that she and her students use. She says that you can use it for channelings, private sessions of any kind, or personal connections with Vywamus. She says that this invocation is especially powerful immediately before bedtime, or when you desire a personal communication at a higher vibration.

Vywamus is electrical, and his color is blue. During this process, you may feel a tingling in your arms, hands, or legs. You may experience electricity moving through you. You may have a sense of spiraling, or see the color electrical blue. Remember, we're electromagnetic beings, so you're safe. If for any reason you feel uncomfortable, just ask that the process be made comfortable for your physical being.

First, close your eyes and focus on your breath. Bring your attention within your being. Imagine that you're bringing in from the Universe a cloud of electrical blue. Add some white, and if you like, some soft pink. Allow this blue cloud to surround you so that you can feel yourself completely within it. Take your time with this process so that you feel cocooned in the electrical blue cloud.

When you're ready, state your intent to channel Vywamus. For example:

> "Vywamus, I'm open to channel your energy and to receive your guidance."

You can ask any question you wish. Please keep in mind that Vywamus does not work as a psychic, but rather a highly evolved spiritual teacher.

Yogananda
(India, North America)

Paramahansa Yogananda was an Indian yogi born in 1893. In 1920, at his teacher Babaji's request, Yogananda traveled to America to introduce the Western world to the practice of Kriya yoga. He wrote the popular book *Autobiography of a Yogi* and opened Self-Realization Fellowship (SRF) centers worldwide. Yogananda's centers, books, and teachings blend Eastern and Western spirituality, and many of his writings quote Jesus Christ as an example of love, compassion, and forgiveness. (In fact, Jesus is one of the six gurus of SRF, the other five being Yogananda, Krishna, Babaji, Lahiri Mahasaya, and Sri Yukteswar.) Yogananda, like Babaji, teaches that all religions have an underlying unity.

Yogananda's legacy includes bringing yoga to North America and introducing Westerners to meditation and chanting. All of his teachings focused upon developing loving connections and communication with God; and living a happy, healthy life.

Yogananda passed physically from the world in 1952, but he continues to teach, heal, and guide people as one of the newer ascended masters.

My dear friend Michael Wise, lead singer for the band Angel Earth, wrote down his accounts of working with Yogananda, and sent me the story just two months before he passed away. Now Michael is with his beloved Yogananda.

"My experience with Guruji Paramahansa Yogananda began in the spring of 1992 when his book *Autobiography of a Yogi* literally fell off of the shelf of a local bookstore into my hands. I purchased the book and was enthralled with its contents. I then began studying Yogananda's Kriya Yoga meditation technique through his Self-Realization Fellowship.

"It was in the early morning, 4:30 A.M. of a winter's day in 1994, during my daily meditation routine before going to work, that I reached a very loving and sacred place. My diligent practice and trust in Yogananda's teachings brought me to a level of meditation that I'd never before known. In what seemed like an instant, I was transported to a place of serene beauty: a sun room with a huge arching window overlooking a garden rich in colorful flowers, trees, and sunlight as bright as I'd ever seen. I just stood in silence amazed at the sight, sound, and feeling of the experience.

"Then, just to the left of the window, I noticed a small table with four chairs around it. In the chair to my left and the one at the back of the table, two figures appeared. They were moving and seemed very alive, and then they came into sharper focus. I was very startled as I recognized one of them to be Yogananda himself! He looked up at me and smiled, then I heard a voice call my name—it was the other figure, who suddenly came into focus. *'Michael,'* the voice said, and then I recognized the other figure to be Jesus! Jesus called my name again and smiled and gently said to me, *'Be as a child at play.'*

"Yogananda then leaned forward and added, *'. . . and continue to study my lessons!'* Both smiled at me. I was then gently returned to my place in my basement studio in my home. The experience is still very vivid in my memory as I write this in May of 2002. Both Yogananda and Jesus have been with me every step of the way of my awakening to the Spirit within. They're with me now and always will be as we share this experience of transformation here on Earth."

Helps with:

- Clear communication with God
- Divine love
- Healing—spiritual, emotional, and physical
- Peace, personal and global
- Unity of religious beliefs
- Yoga practice

Invocation

Yogananda is actively and deeply involved with world affairs, and comes to anyone who desires to bring peace to the planet. The best way to reach Yogananda is through meditation. Meditate while mentally repeating the word *love* and simultaneously holding the intention of contacting him. You may then see a mental vision of Yogananda and have the experience of conversing with him. During this conversation, you could ask Yogananda for Divine direction about your spiritual path or any other question or concern you may have.

PART II

Invocations for Specific Needs and Issues

Prayers to Connect with Multiple Divinities, for Specific Needs

The suggested prayers listed here are just that: suggested. They simply represent one of many ways to invoke the deities who oversee the situation with which you need help. You may wish to try out these invocations as they're printed first and then take note of the results. Then, in subsequent prayers, modify the wording as your inner guidance directs.

You don't need to use fancy or poetic verbiage to invoke the divinities. All you need to do is mentally say their names and ask them for help with whatever issue, problem, or situation you're concerned about. You can use the list in Part III to quickly research which divinities specialize in the particular area you're interested in. It's better to say a simple prayer as soon as you notice you need assistance, instead of trying to come up with the "perfect" prayer. The sooner we call for help, the easier a situation is to resolve. This is similar to calling the fire department at the first sign of smoke instead of waiting until it's turned into an uncontrollable blaze.

When you say these prayers, it's important to hold in mind the question or situation for which you're seeking help. You can either say the prayers mentally or speak them aloud. These prayers are even more effective if you can hold them in your hand, so you might want to photocopy the pages from this book that the applicable prayers are on, or handwrite them. Say each prayer three times, with full conscious awareness of each word, and then put the printed prayer in a special place such as on your altar, on an inside window ledge facing the moonlight, or beneath your pillow or bed.

When you're done saying a prayer, thank the divinities for their help. Mentally check in with them often. They're available to you while your situation is being resolved, so it's wise to seek counsel from them, talk to them about your successes or challenges, and ask them questions.

Remember, you cannot bother a divinity, and you're not pulling them off of something or someone more important. You and your situation are of vital importance to them, now and always. They're able to be with everyone who calls upon them simultaneously; and they can have a unique, personalized experience with each person. Ascended masters and archangels have no limiting beliefs, so they have no time or space restrictions. It's their great pleasure to help you, because when *you're* at peace, the world is one person closer to being peaceful as a whole.

Abundance

To increase your supply of money, food, time, opportunities, or whatever you desire more of, here's a powerful prayer. As you say this prayer, utter each name slowly, feeling the energy of each name:

> *"Beloved Abundantia . . . Damara . . . Dana . . . Ganesh . . . Lakshmi . . . and Sedna . . . thank you for the abundant supply in my life, overflowing with beautiful opportunities for me to express my Divine light so that others may benefit as well. Thank you for the peace, happiness, and love you bring me. Thank you for all of the time and energy that I have to fulfill my dreams and desires. Thank you for the abundant financial support and supply. I gratefully accept all of your gifts, and ask that you keep them coming."*

Addictions and Cravings

If you're truly ready to release a substance, craving, or addictive pattern from your life, this is a very powerful method. After saying this prayer, you'll likely find that all cravings are gone. Or, you might have one last binge-for-the-road, which leads you to give up the addiction for good.

First, imagine that the item, person, or situation that you want to release is sitting on your lap. Then imagine that it's floating in front of your navel. See or feel all of the cords, webs, and roots extending from your navel to the items you're releasing. Then say this prayer:

"Archangel Raphael, beloved angel of healing!
Babaji, teacher of overcoming the physical world!
Beloved Devi, who cares so deeply!
Shining Maat, bringer of Divine light!
Serapis Bey, overseer of ascension!
Please cut the cords of addictions and cravings from me.
I now fully release any and all patterns of addictions, and
I completely embrace my freedom and physical health."

Clairvoyance

This prayer can help you open, or increase, your ability to see psychically. For extra clairvoyant power, hold a clear quartz crystal up to your third eye (the area between your two eyebrows) while saying this prayer:

"Divine light, please enter my third eye and fill it with illumination, clarity, and the ability to clearly see across the veil. Powerful Apollo, I thank you for opening my third eye! Archangels Haniel, Jeremiel, Raphael, and Raziel, I thank you for your magical Divine energies and assistance with my spiritual sight now! Victorious Horus, thank you for stationing your eye in front of my own, so that I may see multidimensionally like you! Beloved Kuan Yin, I thank you for sending me energy from your third eye to my own so that I may see love in everything and everyone! Dearest Sulis, thank you for invoking the power of my clairvoyant energy! I thank you all for fully opening me up to see truth, beauty, light, and eternal life!"

Clear Communication with God

This powerful prayer can help you clear away blocks so that you can more clearly hear God and your Divine guidance:

> *"God, I deeply desire a closer relationship and clearer communication with You. I ask for Your assistance in opening me up so that I can clearly hear, see, feel, and know Your messages for me. Jesus . . . Moses . . . Babaji . . . Yogananda . . . you demonstrated the ability to clearly hear God during your lifetimes on Earth. I ask your assistance in teaching me your ways. Please work with me so that I'm fully open to hearing God's messages and that I trust what I hear. Thank you, God. Thank you, Jesus. Thank you, Moses. Thank you, Babaji. Thank you, Yogananda."*

Connecting with the Fairies

If you'd like to see fairies, or at least feel a greater connection with them, try saying this prayer while outdoors. It's especially powerful to say it, mentally or aloud, while you're in an area where wildflowers grow. You'll know that you've successfully made the connection with the fairies when you feel compelled to pick up litter in the outdoors. This is one of the first communications that fairies normally make with humans. If you pick up litter, and treat animals and the environment with great respect, the fairies will show their appreciation by granting you wishes.

> *"Beloved Dana, goddess of the leprechauns; beautiful Diana, mistress of the wood nymphs; powerful Maeve, queen of the fairies; golden Oonagh, protector of the fairies: I ask your assistance in connecting with the elemental world. Please introduce me to the fairies, and ask them on my behalf how I can get to know them better. I would like to develop a connection to the fairies and elementals, and I ask that you show me the way. Please help my*

mind and spiritual vision to be open to communications from their magical realm. Thank you."

Courage

If you feel worried, anxious, afraid, or vulnerable, this prayer can give you more courage *and* protect you and your loved ones from harm.

"Powerful protectors from Heaven. Powerful allies by my side! I need your strength, courage, and protection beside me. Please come to me now!

Thank you, Archangel Michael, for giving me the courage to move forward fearlessly.

Thank you, Ashtar, for protecting me in all ways.

Thank you, Brigit, for helping me be a loving warrior on behalf of my beliefs.

Thank you, Cordelia, for removing stress and tension from my mind and body.

Thank you, Green Tara, for bringing me rapid results to my prayers.

Thank you, Horus, for helping me clearly see the truth of this situation.

Thank you, Kali, for helping me stand my ground.

Thank you, Moses, for helping me be a fearless leader.

Thank you, Saint-Germain, for helping me stay positive, cheerful, and optimistic.

Thank you all for being with me and helping me rise up to, and rise above, all illusions of problems. Thank you for helping me grow and learn from all challenges. Thank you for reminding me to breathe and be centered in peacefulness!"

Finding Your Life's Purpose

Here's a prayer to help you discover your overall life's purpose, as well as get direction about the next step to take. Your prayer will likely be answered with a combination of Divine guidance and signs. Divine guidance includes internal messages such as feelings, thoughts, ideas, and visions that tell you what your heart truly desires. Signs are repetitious messages that you see or overhear coming from sources other than yourself, such as a phrase that you continually see on posters, in newspapers, or that you hear people say. It's best to write down these inner and outer messages and look for a constant theme that will direct you to your next step . . . and overall purpose.

"Archangel Michael . . . Jesus . . . Saint-Germain . . . and Vywamus . . . you can see what is the best next step for me to take. I need to hear, feel, and see this information clearly. I need to have faith in taking this next step. I need to feel courage and excitement about this next step. Thank you for supplying me with information, encouragement, and motivation.

"Archangel Chamuel . . . Brigit . . . Saint Francis . . . Thoth . . . and my higher self . . . beloved and Divine teammates in my life purpose, I am grateful for your clear guidance about my life purpose. I am grateful because I truly believe that I deserve happiness, success, and abundance. I am grateful to know that I am worthy of receiving your help and support. Thank you, God. Thank you, divinities. Thank you all."

Finding Your Soulmate

If you desire a spiritually based romantic relationship, then say this prayer. You can amplify the power of the prayer by first imagining the feeling of being in such a relationship. Imagine that you're with your soulmate and are completely loved and honored. Then say:

"Love gods and goddesses sent from Heaven above; Aengus and Aphrodite, male and female deities signifying beauty and loveliness; Guinevere and Isolt, bringers of magical love: I invite you to my spiritual wedding, wherein I am wed to my soulmate first in spiritual union. I feel my beloved deeply within my body and soul. I send this feeling to my soulmate, and I thank you for delivering these feelings to my beloved as my sacred Valentine message. Thank you for uniting my soulmate and me through the ethers. Thank you for clearly guiding us to find one another. Thank you for bringing us together in blissful union. Thank you for overseeing my love life."

Global Peace

These divinities are already watching over the world, keeping war at bay, and talking with world leaders about peace. Our prayers add a great deal to the momentum of global peace. Each prayer adds so much, is definitely powerful, and is very needed. On behalf of the rest of us who live on this planet, thank you for saying this prayer (or one like it) on a regular basis:

"God is peace . . . God is everywhere . . . therefore, peace is everywhere, in truth. This is the truth. And I thank You, God, for this truth. Thank You for sending your ministers of peace to watch over us now and always. Thank you, Archangel Chamuel, for helping all of us find inner peace. Thank you, Buddha, for being the embodiment of peace. Thank you, Forseti, for successfully resolving conflict peacefully. Thank you, Kuan Ti, for your wise counsel with world leaders. Thank you, Maitreya, for replacing all anger with joy. Thank you, Saint Francis, for helping us stay devoted to God's peace. Thank you, Jesus, for overseeing humanity. Thank you, Serapis Bey, for helping us all live at our highest potential. Thank you, Yogananda, for helping us feel Divinely loved."

If war is pending, or has already broken out, then say this prayer:

"Archangel Michael, I ask that you intervene in this situation to the degree that it is affecting me. Please release the spirits and lower energies in this area, and take them to the light for healing and transmutation. Ashtar, please watch over our planet and ensure its peace, balance, and intactness. Athena, please intervene to the degree that this situation involves me, and work with the world leaders toward alternatives to war. Ishtar, please help the people to show leadership and strength. Kuan Ti, please help us all have the foresight to know the effects tomorrow of our actions today. Thank you, heavenly leaders. Thank you, God. Thank you for the peace surrounding and within this world. Thank you for the peace within the hearts of everyone, everywhere."

You can add to this prayer a visualization of Archangel Michael holding a vacuum above the planet, lifting up all negative energy from any geographical areas experiencing conflict.

Healing a Child

If a child is in need of healing or relief from pain, then say this prayer. It's been said that when parents pray on behalf of their children, those prayers are answered first in Heaven.

I also recommend handwriting the prayer and placing it face up on a cabinet or shelf in the child's bedroom. If the child is old enough to say prayers, ask the child to say the prayer with you:

"Thank you, God, for my child's perfect health. Thank you for peace within my child's body. Thank you, Archangel Raphael, for your powerful healing energy, which heals everything rapidly with each breath my child takes. Thank you, Damara, for gently comforting and reassuring me and my child. Thank you, Hathor, for clearly instructing me on how I can best help my child. Thank you,

Mother Mary, for watching over all of us and sending us your Divine healing love."

Healing a Pet

If your cat, dog, or other animal has a physical challenge, then you'll want to call upon the great animal healers in Heaven to help and heal. As you say this prayer, either look at your pet in the flesh or in your mind, or gaze at a photo of your beloved furry friend:

"Healers in Heaven, I love [name of pet] *with all my heart. Please join my love with yours and send it to* [name of pet]. *Dearest Aine, I ask that you surround my pet with your bright silver energy of peace and happiness. Dearest Raphael, I ask that you encircle my pet with your emerald-green energy of health and wellness. Dearest Dana, I ask that you help my pet's system to be balanced and in its natural state of vitality. Dearest Saint Francis, I ask that you communicate with my pet and let me know what I can do to bring my pet comfort.*

"Thank you, Aine . . . Raphael . . . Dana . . . Saint Francis . . . for your healing work. Thank you for my pet's perfect health. Thank you for my pet's comfort. Thank you for lifting our spirits. I now surrender this situation to you and God with complete faith and confidence."

Healing for Oneself

If you experience a physical challenge, it's comforting to know that you have access to powerful healers. This prayer can supplement any other spiritual or medical treatment you're implementing:

"Beloved Jesus, loving healer of God . . . beloved Aine, loving healer of God . . . beloved Archangel Raphael, loving healer of God

. . . beloved Archangel Zadkiel, loving healer of God . . . beloved Saint Therese, loving healer of God. The love of God is now inside of me. I am completely filled and healed with the love of God. Jesus . . . Aine . . . Raphael . . . Zadkiel . . . Therese . . . I am so grateful for the ministering, healing, and comfort that you bring to me . . . thank you for surrounding and filling me completely with positive energy. Thank you for clearing and cleaning me completely. I am now completely well. I now feel absolutely wonderful, filled with the spirit of love in all ways. I am energized. I am happy. I am rested and refreshed. Thank You, God. Thank you, Divine healers."

Protection and Guidance for Your Child

If you're worried about your child, say this prayer of protection and guidance to ease your mind, and to help protect and guide your child:

"Dana . . . Hathor . . . Ishtar . . . Mother Mary . . . mothering goddesses and teachers of parents, I surrender my worries to you. Please nurture my child and this situation [describe your concerns] *so that we may all be joyful and feel peace. Please teach me how to best guide my child. Please direct my words and actions so that I speak my truth in a way that my child will hear. Please help me stay centered in faith and courage.*

"Archangel Michael . . . Artemis . . . Kuan Yin . . . Vesta . . . powerful protectors of children, I ask that you closely watch over my child [say your child's name]. *Thank you for closely monitoring and protecting my child. Thank you for ensuring my child's safety, happiness, and health. Thank you for guiding my child in a direction that brings about blessings, wellness, meaning, and abundance. Thank you, Dana . . . Hathor. . . Ishtar . . . Mother Mary . . . Archangel Michael . . . Artemis . . . Kuan Yin . . . Vesta . . . for protecting and guiding my child. I am truly grateful."*

Resolving Conflict

If you've had a disagreement with someone, or you're in the middle of a conflict of some kind, then it's a good idea to ask for help from the divinities. This prayer isn't to help you win or to get the other person to apologize. It's simply to create peace and forgiveness all the way around:

"Beloved helpers in Heaven, please come to me now . . . Archangel Raguel, heavenly minister of fairness . . . Athena, goddess of peaceful solutions . . . Forseti, overseer of truth and justice . . . Guardian angels of [name the person or persons involved in the conflict] *. . . I thank you for your intervention. I ask that you deliver my message to everyone involved in this situation and let them know of my desire for peace. I ask for a peaceful and rapid resolution, and I surrender this entire situation to you and God, knowing that it is already resolved. I know that only peace exists in truth, and that peace is everywhere, including within this situation and within everyone involved. Please clearly guide me as to my role in this peaceful resolution. Thank you."*

Weight Loss

Healthy weight loss involves exercise and healthful eating. This prayer can boost your motivation to exercise, and reduce your cravings for high-fat foods:

"Heaven, help me stay fit and toned, and be a healthy weight. I ask that the powerful spiritual motivators and coaches please come to me now. Apollo . . . Oonagh . . . Serapis Bey . . . I need your masterful help. Please increase my desire to exercise. Please help me find an exercise program that easily fits my schedule, budget, and interests. Please help me take the first step. Please help me get the support of my family so that I may exercise with their blessings.

Please help me see results so that I may stay encouraged.

"Archangel Raphael . . . Babaji . . . Devi . . . Maat . . . I now surrender to you my cravings for high-fat and sugary foods. . . . You know which foods and drinks are healthful and which are not for my body. I ask that you adjust my cravings so that I only desire healthful foods and drinks. Please increase my motivation to eat light, nutritious foods. Please increase my motivation to drink light, natural beverages.

"Thank you for overseeing my physical health and well-being."

PART III

A List of Whom to Call Upon for Specific Needs

Calling Upon Archangels
and Ascended Masters

W hen a specific need arises, turn to the list on the following pages so that you'll know which archangels and ascended masters to call upon. You can use this information in many ways. For instance, you can place your hand over the divinities' names listed under your specific need. As you hold your hand there, think the thought, *Beloved Divinities, I need your help, love, and assistance with* [describe the particular situation]. *Thank you for this Divine intervention.*

You can also take the list and look up and read about each Divinity in Part I. In that way, your knowledge of the archangel or ascended master deepens. The combination of having personal experiences and interaction with a Divinity, along with reading about that being's history and background, makes for a rich relationship.

A quick way to deal with an issue is to look at the list corresponding to your situation and say each being's name as you do your prayer or even sing it. The intention of your prayer is more important than the words or method. The divinities hear your prayerful intention, and they respond with love immediately. No prayer is denied or ignored. After all, the archangels and ascended masters help us because they're enacting God's plan of peace on Earth, one person at a time. If they can help you to find peace through their Divine intervention into some Earthly situation, then it's their sacred pleasure to do so.

This list covers a broad range of human needs and situations. If you don't see a listing for your specific situation, then find one that closely matches it. You can also pray for guidance as to which Divinity would be most appropriate for your cause.

Abundance
Abundantia
Coventina
Damara
Dana
Ganesh
Lakshmi
Sedna

>   Emergency Supply
> • Aeracura
> • Green Tara

Addictions, help with
Archangel Raphael
Babaji
Devi
Maat
Serapis Bey

Aesthetics
Lakshmi

Airline Pilots and Crew
Saint Therese

Alchemy
Archangel Raziel
Archangel Uriel
Dana
Lugh
Maeve
Merlin
Saint-Germain

Animals
>   Breeding, Pregnancy, and Birthing
> • Diana

>   Communication
> • Saint Francis

>   Finding Lost Pets
> • Archangel Raphael

>   Healing
> • Aine
> • Archangel Raphael
> • Dana
> • Saint Francis

>   Horses, healing and protecting
> • Maeve

>   Protecting
> • Aine
> • Archangel Ariel
> • Artemis
> • Sedna

Answered Prayers
Archangel Sandalphon
Jesus
Kuan Yin

Arguments, resolving
Archangel Raguel
Athena
Forseti

Aromatherapy
Maeve

Artists and Artistic Projects
Aeracura
Archangel Gabriel
Archangel Jophiel
Athena
Ganesh
Hathor
Lugh
Serapis Bey

Ascension
Serapis Bey

Attractiveness
Aphrodite
Hathor
Maeve
Oonagh

Aura-Soma Therapy
Melchizedek

Authority Figures—dealing with them fearlessly
Moses
Saint-Germain

Balance
Buddha

Beautiful Thoughts
Archangel Jophiel

Beauty
Aphrodite
Archangel Jophiel
Hathor
Isis
Lakshmi
Maeve
Oonagh

Blessings
Krishna
Sulis

Blindness
Jesus
Saint Padre Pio

Breakups, healing from
Isolt

Breathwork
Babaji

Cabala, studying and understanding
Solomon

Camping
Artemis

Career
Archangel Chamuel
Lu-Hsing

Celebration
Cordelia
Hathor

Ceremonies
Nemetona

Chakra Clearing
Archangel Michael
Melchizedek

Children
Adoption
- Archangel Gabriel
- Artemis
- Mother Mary

Attention Deficit Disorder (ADD or ADHD)
- Archangel Metatron

Childbirth, painless
- Diana

Conception and Fertility
- Aine
- Archangel Gabriel
- Artemis
- Dana
- Hathor
- Ishtar
- Mother Mary

Crystal Children
- Archangel Metatron
- Mother Mary

Custody
- Damara

Determining Gender of Unborn Baby
- Archangel Sandalphon

Guiding
- Damara

Healing
- Archangel Raphael
- Damara
- Jesus
- Mother Mary
- Saint Therese

Indigo Children
- Archangel Metatron
- Melchizedek
- Mother Mary

In General
- Archangel Metatron
- Artemis
- Kuan Yin
- Mother Mary

Mother-Son Relationship
- Horus
- Mother Mary

Overcoming Acting-Out
Behavior
- Saint Francis

Parenting
- Dana
- Hathor
- Ishtar
- Mother Mary

Protection
- Archangel Michael
- Artemis
- Kuan Yin
- Melchizedek
- Vesta

Those Who Professionally
Help Children
- Archangel Metatron
- Mother Mary

Twins
- Diana

Clairvoyance, increasing
Apollo
Archangel Haniel
Archangel Jeremiel
Archangel Raphael
Archangel Raziel
Horus
Kuan Yin
Sulis

Clear Communication with God
Babaji
Jesus
Moses
Yogananda

Clear Thinking and Clarification
Maat

Commitment
    To a Love Relationship
- Aphrodite

    To One's Beliefs
- Archangel Michael
- Maat

Compassion
Archangel Zadkiel
Ishtar
Kuan Yin
Tara

Cooperation from Other People
Archangel Raguel

Cosmetics
Hathor

Courage
Archangel Michael
Ashtar
Brigit
Cordelia
Horus
Kali
Moses
Saint-Germain
Green Tara

Crafts and Craftspeople
Athena
Lugh

Cravings, eliminating or reducing
Apollo
Archangel Raphael

Crystals
Melchizedek
Merlin

Dancing
Hathor
Oonagh

Decision-Making
El Morya
Hathor

Defending the Unfairly Treated
Archangel Raguel

Determination
Kali

Detoxification
Archangel Raphael
Devi
Melchizedek

Direction
Archangel Michael
Jesus
Saint-Germain
Vywamus

Divination
Merlin
Thoth

Divine Guidance
Jesus
Moses
Oonagh

Divine Light
Vesta

Divine Love
Jesus
Yogananda

Divine Magic
Archangel Ariel
Archangel Raziel
Dana
Isis
Lugh
Maat
Merlin
Solomon
Thoth

Divorce
Healing from
• Isolt

Making Decisions about
• Damara

Dolphins
Coventina
Sedna

Dreams
Archangel Jeremiel
Sedna

Earth Changes
Archangel Uriel
Ashtar
Melchizedek

Ego, overcoming
Buddha
Jesus
Moses
Sanat Kumara

Elementals (fairies, leprechauns, etc.); seeing, hearing, and connecting with
Dana
Diana
Maeve
Oonagh

Emergency Money
Aeracura
Green Tara

Employment
Lu-Hsing

Empowerment
Archangel Raguel
Pele

Encouragement
Vywamus

Energy
Archangel Michael
Pele
Sanat Kumara

Energy Work and Healing
Melchizedek
Merlin

Engagement (in a love relationship)
Aphrodite

Environmental Concerns
Aine
Archangel Ariel
Artemis
Coventina
Saint Francis

Esoteric Information
Archangel Raziel
Ashtar
Melchizedek

Exercise
Apollo
Oonagh
Serapis Bey

Extraterrestrials
Ashtar

Eyesight
Archangel Raphael
Horus
Jesus
Saint Padre Pio
Sulis

Fairness
Forseti

Faith, increasing
Aine
Archangel Raphael
El Morya
Jesus
Moses

Family

Divorce Involving Children
- Damara

Harmony
- Archangel Raguel
- Damara

Femininity

Aphrodite

Feminine Power and Strength

Artemis

Brigit

Isis

Kali

Maeve

Pele

Feng Shui

Melchizedek

Financial Investments

Abundantia

Fingers, healing

Sedna

Fire Control

Vesta

Flowers

Cordelia

Krishna

Saint Therese

Focus

Kali

Kuthumi

Saint-Germain

Food

Abundant Supply
- Jesus
- Lakshmi
- Sedna

Purifying and Spiritualizing
- Krishna

Forgiveness

Archangel Zadkiel

Jesus

Saint Padre Pio

Freedom for Falsely Accused Prisoners and Prisoners-of-War

Kuan Ti

Gardening
Cordelia
Krishna
Saint Therese
Sulis

Gentleness
Ishtar
Kuan Yin

Goal-Setting and Achievement
Pele
Saint-Germain

Good Fortune
Abundantia

Grace
Archangel Haniel

Gracefulness
Aphrodite

Grieving, comfort and healing for
Archangel Azrael

Groundedness
El Morya

Hands, healing
Sedna

Happiness, lasting
Lakshmi

Happy Endings
Apollo
Archangel Uriel

Harmony
In Families
- Archangel Raguel
- Damara

In General
- Archangel Uriel

In Groups
- Archangel Raguel

While Traveling
- Archangel Raphael

Healers, guidance and support for
Archangel Raphael
Jesus
Melchizedek
Saint John of God
Saint Padre Pio

Healing

Abilities
- Archangel Haniel
- Archangel Raphael
- Jesus
- Maeve
- Saint Padre Pio

Addictions
- Archangel Raphael
- Babaji
- Devi
- Maat
- Serapis Bey

Animals
- Aine
- Archangel Ariel
- Archangel Raphael

Blindness
- Jesus
- Saint Padre Pio

Cardiovascular and Heart
- Saint John of God

Eyesight
- Archangel Raphael
- Jesus
- Saint Padre Pio
- Sulis

From Grief
- Archangel Azrael

From Relationship Breakup, Divorce, or Separation
- Isolt

Hands and Fingers
- Sedna

Horses
- Maeve

In General
- Archangel Raphael
- Ishtar
- Jesus
- Saint John of God
- Saint Padre Pio
- Saint Therese
- Sanat Kumara
- Vywamus
- Yogananda

Menopause
- Maeve

People Emotionally
- Archangel Zadkiel
- Jesus
- Lugh
- Saint John of God
- Vywamus

People Physically
- Aine
- Archangel Raphael
- Archangel Zadkiel
- Jesus
- Saint John of God
- Saint Therese

People Who Are Hospitalized
for Mental or Physical
Reasons
• Saint John of God

Premenstrual Syndrome
(PMS)
• Maeve

Relationships
• Aine

With Aromatherapy
• Maeve

With Aura-Soma
• Melchizedek

With Crystals
• Merlin
• Melchizedek
• Saint-Germain

With Energy Work
• Merlin
• Melchizedek

With Water
• Coventina
• Sulis

Healthful Eating
Apollo

Hiking
Artemis

Home
Money for Household Needs
• Damara
• Lakshmi

Space Clearing the Back- and
Front-Yard Area
• Nemetona

Space Clearing the Home
Interior
• Archangel Michael
• Archangel Raphael
• Artemis
• Kuan Ti
• Kuan Yin
• Lakshmi
• Saint-Germain
• Saint John of God
• Sanat Kumara
• Solomon
• Vesta

Humor
• Maitreya

**Hurricanes, diverting and
dispelling**
Sedna

Inspiration
Vywamus

Integrity
Maat

Interior Decorating
Archangel Jophiel

Intuition, increasing
Artemis
Sedna

Inventors
Aeracura

Job Interviews
Lu-Hsing

Journalism
Archangel Gabriel

Joy
Aine
Buddha
Cordelia
Isis
Maitreya
Saint John of God

Justice, attaining
Athena
Ida-Ten

Kindness
Kuan Yin
Mother Mary

Labyrinths
Archangel Raziel
Melchizedek
Nemetona
Solomon

Laughter
Maitreya

Leadership
Melchizedek
Moses

Legal Matters, resolving
Forseti
Ida-Ten
Kuan Ti

Lesbian Concerns
Diana

Life Changes
Archangel Jeremiel
Cordelia

Melchizedek
Saint-Germain
Solomon

Life Purpose
Archangel Chamuel
Archangel Michael
Brigit
Kuthumi
Saint Francis
Saint-Germain
Thoth
Vywamus

Marriage
Aphrodite
Ishtar

Mathematics
Melchizedek
Thoth

Longevity
White Tara

Meaning in Life, increasing
Devi
Saint Francis

Lost Items, finding
Archangel Chamuel
Archangel Zadkiel

Mechanical Problems, fixing
Apollo
Archangel Michael

Love, receiving and giving
Kuan Yin
Maitreya

Medicine Wheels
Nemetona

Mediation of Disputes
Archangel Raguel

Manifesting
Aeracura
Archangel Ariel
Archangel Raziel
Babaji
Damara
Jesus

Meditation
Buddha
Jesus
Yogananda

Memory Enhancement
Archangel Zadkiel
Kuthumi

Menopause
Maeve

Menstrual Cycle
Maeve

Mercy
Kuan Yin
Mother Mary

Miracles
Jesus
Moses

Money
Abundantia
Damara
Dana
Ganesh
Lakshmi
Sedna

> Emergency Supply
> • Aeracura
> • Green Tara

Moon Energy
Archangel Haniel

Motivation
> For Life Purpose
> • Archangel Michael
> • Kuthumi
> • Vywamus

> To Eat Healthfully
> • Apollo
> • Archangel Michael

> To Exercise
> • Apollo
> • Oonagh
> • Serapis Bey

Music and Musicians
Aengus
Archangel Gabriel
Archangel Sandalphon
Hathor
Kuan Yin
Lugh
Serapis Bey

**Newly Deceased Loved Ones
(help and comfort for their
souls)**
Archangel Azrael

**Obstacles, avoiding and
overcoming**
Ganesh
Tara

Orderliness and Organization
Archangel Metatron
Archangel Raguel
Kuthumi
Maat

Parties
Hathor

Passion, increasing
Aengus
Aine
Aphrodite
Isolt
Pele
Vesta

Peace
Global
- Archangel Chamuel
- Babaji
- Buddha
- Forseti
- Kuan Ti
- Maitreya
- Saint Francis
- Serapis Bey
- Yogananda

Household
- Ganesh

Personal
- Babaji
- Buddha
- Forseti
- Kuthumi
- Lakshmi
- Maitreya
- Saint Francis
- Serapis Bey
- Yogananda

Perseverance
Kuthumi
Saint-Germain

Physical Fitness
Apollo
Oonagh
Serapis Bey

Pilots
Saint Therese

Playfulness
Aine

Poetry
Lugh

Poise
Archangel Haniel

Pregnancy

Determining Gender of
Unborn Baby
- Archangel Sandalphon

Harmonious
- Hathor

Painless Childbirth
- Diana

Twins
- Diana

Premenstrual Syndrome (PMS)
Maeve

Prioritizing
Pele

Procrastination, overcoming
Archangel Michael
Pele
Vywamus

Promotions at Work
Lu-Hsing

Prophecies about World Events
Kuan Ti

Prophetic Abilities, increasing
Apollo
Archangel Jeremiel
Merlin
Serapis Bey
Thoth

Protection

Against Deceit and
Manipulation
- Maat

Against Psychic Attack
- Athena
- El Morya
- Ishtar
- Melchizedek
- Saint-Germain

From Lower Energies
- Archangel Michael
- Ishtar

From Religious or Spiritual
Persecution
- Babaji
- Ida-Ten

In General
- Archangel Michael
- Artemis
- Ashtar
- Athena
- Brigit
- Kali
- Lugh
- Tara

Legal
- Forseti
- Ida-Ten

Of Animals
- Aine
- Archangel Ariel
- Artemis
- Maeve

Of Children in Particular
- Artemis
- Kuan Yin
- Vesta

Of Oceans and Lakes from Pollution
- Archangel Ariel
- Sedna

Of Spiritual Centers
- Ida-Ten

Of Travelers and Their Luggage
- Archangel Raphael

Of Valuables
- Abundantia

Of Women in Particular
- Aine
- Artemis
- Brigit
- Kuan Yin

Psychic Abilities, increasing
Apollo
Archangel Haniel
Archangel Raziel
Coventina
Kuan Ti
Merlin
Thoth

Purification and Cleanliness
Coventina
Maat

Radio Careers, Interviews— dealing with
Archangel Gabriel

Raises in Salary
Lu-Hsing

Recordkeeping
Archangel Metatron

Relationships
All Aspects
- Devi
- Ishtar
- Krishna
- Oonagh

Attracting
- Aengus
- Aphrodite
- Guinevere
- Isolt

Breakups, Divorce, and
Separation, healing from
- Isolt

Building and Strengthening
- Archangel Chamuel
Commitment
- Aphrodite

Healing
- Aine

Honest Communication
- Pele

Increasing Warmth Within
- Brigit
- Vesta

Lesbian
- Diana

Marriage
- Ishtar

Mother-Son
- Horus

Romance
Aengus
Aphrodite
Guinevere
Isolt
Krishna

Sacred Geometry
Thoth

Sailing
Sedna

Self-Esteem
Archangel Michael
Dana
Diana
Isis

Sexuality
Aphrodite
Ishtar
Pele

Shape-Shifting
Merlin

Simplifying Your Life
Babaji

Slowing Down from a Hectic Pace
Archangel Jophiel

Solutions to Difficulties
Apollo
Archangel Michael
Archangel Uriel
Jesus
Lugh

Soulmate Relationships, finding
Aengus
Archangel Chamuel
Hathor

Spirit Releasement
Archangel Michael
Archangel Raphael
Kuan Ti
Melchizedek
Sanat Kumara
Solomon

Spirituality
Awakening
• Krishna

Devotion
• Saint Francis

Enlightenment
• Buddha
• Kuan Yin

• Sanat Kumara
• White Tara

Growth
• Babaji
• Buddha
• Saint Padre Pio

Understanding
• Archangel Metatron
• Archangel Uriel
• Ashtar
• Buddha
• Jesus
• Sanat Kumara
• Solomon
• Green Tara

Sports
Apollo

Standing Your Ground
Horus

Strength
Horus

Stress Management
Cordelia

Students and Studying
Archangel Uriel
Archangel Zadkiel

Support
    <u>For Those Who Are Grieving</u>
    • Archangel Azrael

Swimming
Coventina
Sedna

Talents, discovering
Archangel Michael
Vywamus

Teaching
Archangel Metatron
Archangel Michael
Mother Mary
Thoth

Television Careers, Interviews—dealing with
Archangel Gabriel

Tenacity
Kali

Time-Warping
Merlin

Travelers (protection, orderliness, and harmony)
Archangel Raphael
Ganesh

Truth
Forseti
Ida-Ten
Maat

Twins
Diana

Unity of all Religious Beliefs
Babaji
Yogananda

Valuables, protecting
Abundantia

Vegetarianism
Krishna

Vitality
Archangel Michael

War, avoiding or stopping
Archangel Michael
Ashtar
Athena
Ishtar
Kuan Ti

Warmth—in relationships, body, and environment
Brigit
Vesta

Water

Abundant Supply of
- Coventina

Cleanliness
- Coventina

Protecting the Oceans and Lakes
- Archangel Ariel
- Sedna

Weather

In General
- Archangel Uriel
- Ishtar

Increasing Sunshine
- Apollo

Wedding Ceremonies
Ganesh

Weight Loss
Apollo
Archangel Raphael
Oonagh
Serapis Bey

Whales
Coventina
Sedna

Wisdom
Ganesh
Solomon

Women

Protecting
- Aine
- Archangel Michael
- Artemis

Women's Issues
Guinevere

Worthiness
Archangel Michael
Dana

Writers and Writing Projects
Archangel Gabriel
Archangel Metatron
Archangel Uriel
Athena
Ganesh
Thoth

Yoga Practice
Babaji
Yogananda

APPENDIX

Glossary of Terms

Archangel—A powerful overseer of other angels, and a manager of specialized functions, such as clearing away fear, protecting humans, or healing. Different religions and spiritual groups talk about different numbers of archangels. Some groups claim there are only four, some say seven, and other groups say there are an infinite number.

Ascended Master—A great spiritual teacher or healer who walked upon the Earth as a human, and who continues to help . . . from his or her heavenly home.

Ascension—The process of fully remembering one's unity with God and the one Spirit that unites all people in brother and sisterhood. Those who ascend may bypass the death process, and their entire body may be lifted into Heaven along with their soul. *Ascension* is also a term used for spiritual awakening and enlightenment.

Avatar—A living human who is fully enlightened. Usually, avatars are miracle workers and spiritual teachers.

Bodhisattva—In Buddhism, this term refers to a person who has become enlightened to the point of being eligible for Buddhahood.

Cabala—An ancient Judaic mystical text that discusses secrets of divination and manifestation with symbols, numbers, and wisdom. (Also spelled *Kaballah, Kabalah.*)

Chohan—A term used among Theosophists and in New Age circles to describe an ascended master's specialty. For instance, someone might be a Chohan of love and enlightenment.

Deity—A being who is revered for their spiritual contribution while on Earth, and for their help that continues from the vantage point of Heaven.

Divinity—A being who works directly with the Creator or Universal Force to help Earth and her inhabitants. The terms *deity* and *divinity* can be used interchangeably.

God—When the term appears with a lower-case "g" (god), it means an aspect of the Creator (God)—which has a capital "G." This being has a male energy or identity.

Goddess—An aspect of God the Creator that has a female energy or identity.

Great White Brotherhood—Leaders in Heaven who oversee the safety and spiritual direction of Earth and her inhabitants, and also the light-workers who help upon Earth. The term does not refer to Caucasian males. It comes from the white light that surrounds the members of the council, which includes goddesses.

Lightworkers—A living human who feels called to help Earth and her inhabitants in a way that uses spiritual energy. For instance, a light-worker might feel called upon to engage in healing, teaching, or artistic work to help make the planet a better place.

Shape-Shifting—The ability to take on a markedly different physical appearance. Sometimes this is done at will, sometimes unconsciously.

Space Clearing—Clearing negative energy out of a specific place, such as a home, office, room, temple, backyard, or front yard.

Spirit Releasement—Clearing negative energy out of a person or animal's body and aura.

Triple Goddess—Three aspects of femininity: the virgin, mother, and crone. Triple goddesses have personality or behavior aspects of the virgin, who represents purity, sweetness and innocence. The same goddess may also have a side to her that is the mother, which means she acts matronly and nurturing. A third aspect of the same goddess that may show up is the "crone," which means that she may have a dark and angry side to her, as well as a wise teacher aspect.

Index of Divinities

Bibliography

Ann, Martha and Imel, Dorothy Myers, *Goddesses in World Mythology: A Biographical Dictionary* (Oxford University Press, 1993, Santa Barbara, CA)

Betz, Hans Dieter. (Ed.), *The Greek Magical Papyri in Translation* (The University of Chicago Press, 1986, Chicago)

The Bible, New King James Version

Boucher, Sandy, *Discovering Kwan Yin: Buddhist Goddess of Compassion* (Beacon Press, 1999, Boston)

Brooke, Elisabeth, *Medicine Women: A Pictorial History of Women Healers* (Quest Books, 1997, Wheaton, IL)

Bunson, Matthew, *Angels A to Z: A Who's Who of the Heavenly Host* (Three Rivers Press, New York, 1996)

Cannon, Dolores, *Jesus and the Essenes* (Ozark Mountain Publishing, 1999, Huntsville, AR)

——. *They Walked with Jesus* (Ozark Mountain Publishing, 2000, Huntsville, AR)

Charlesworth, James H. (ed.), *The Old Testament Pseudepigrapha: Apocalyptic Literature & Testaments* (Doubleday, 1983, New York)

Coulter, Charles Russell and Turner, Patricia, *Encyclopedia of Ancient Deities* (McFarland & Company, Inc., 1997, Jefferson, North Carolina)

A Course in Miracles (Foundation for Inner Peace, 1992, Mill Valley, CA)

Craughwell, Thomas J., *Saints for Every Occasion: 101 of Heaven's Most Powerful Patrons* (Stampley Enterprises, Inc., 2001, Charlotte, NC)

Davidson, Gustav, *A Dictionary of Angels: Including the Fallen Angels* (The Free Press, 1967, New York)

Doreal (Translator and Interpretor), *The Emerald Tablets of Thoth-the-Atlantean* (Source Books, Inc., 1996, Nashville, TN)

Epstein, Perle S., *Oriental Mystics and Magicians* (Doubleday, 1975, New York)

Eshelman, James, *The Mystical & Magical System of the A∴A∴ The Spiritual System of Aleister Crowley & George Cecil Jones Step-by-Step* (The College of Thelema, 2000, Los Angeles)

Forrest, M. Isidora, *Isis Magic: Cultivating a Relationship with the Goddess of 10,000 Names* (Llewellyn Publications, 2001, St. Paul, MN)

Hall, Manly P., *The Secret Teaching of All Ages: An Encyclopedic Outline of Masonic, Hermetic, Qabbalistic, and Rosicrucian Symbolical Philosophy* (The Philosophical Research Society)

James, Simon, *The World of the Celts* (Thames and Hudson, 1993, London)

Jones, Kathleen, *Women Saints: Lives of Faith and Courage* (Burns & Oates, 1999, Kent, England)

Johnson, K. Paul, *The Masters Revealed: Madame Blavatsky and the Myth of the Great White Lodge* (State University of New York Press, 1994, Albany)

Jothi, Rev. Dharma, Telephone interview, October 16, 2002

Kyokai, B. D., *The Teaching of Buddha* (Society for the Promotion of Buddhism, 1966, Tokyo)

La Plante, Alice and Clare, *Heaven Help Us: The Worrier's Guide to the Patron Saints* (Dell Publishing, 1999, New York)

Laurence, Richard (translator), *The Book of Enoch the Prophet* (Adventures Unlimited Press, 2000, Kempton, IL)

Lewis, James R., and Oliver, Evelyn Dorothy, *Angels A to Z* (Visible Ink Press, 1996, Detroit)

Lopez, Jr., Donald (ed.), *Religions of China in Practice* (Princeton University Press, 1996, Princeton, NJ)

Makarios, Hieromonk of Simonos Petra, *The Synaxarion: The Lives of Saints of the Orthodox Church*, Vol. 1 (Chalkidike, 1998)

Markale, Jean, *Merlin: Priest of Nature* (Inner Traditions, Int'l., 1995, Rochester, VT)

Mathers, S.L. MacGregor, S.L., *The Key of Solomon the King*, Translated reprint (Samuel Weiser, 1986, York Beach, ME)

Matthews, Caitlin. *The Celtic Book of Days: A Celebration of Celtic Wisdom* (Gill & Macmillan, Ltd., 1995, Dublin, Ireland)

McCoy, Edain, *Celtic Myth & Magick: Harnessing the Power of the Gods and Goddesses* (Llewellyn Publications, 2002, St. Paul, MN)

Monaghan, Patricia, *The New Book of Goddesses and Heroines* (Llewellyn Publications, 2000, St. Paul, MN)

Morgan, James C., *Jesus and Mastership: The Gospel According to Jesus of Nazareth as Dictated Through James Coyle Morgan* (Oakbridge University Press, 1989, Tacoma, WA)

Ronner, John, *Know Your Angels* (Mamre Press, 1993, Murfreesboro, TN)

Runyon, C. P., *The Book of Solomon's Magick* (Church of the Hermetic Sciences, Inc., 2001, Silverado, CA)

"Saint-Germain, comte de," Encyclopaedia Britannica.

Sakya, Jnan B., *Short Descriptions of Gods, Goddesses, and Ritual Objects of Buddhism and Hinduism in Nepal* (Handicraft Association of Nepal, 1998, Kathmandu, Nepal)

Savedow, Steve (Editor and Translator), *Sepher Razial Hemelach: The Book of the Angel Raziel* (Samuel Weiser, Inc., 2000, York Beach, ME)

Starck, Marcia, *Women's Medicine Ways: Cross-Cultural Rites of Passage* (The Crossing Press, 1993, Freedom, CA, 1993)

Stewart, R. J., *Celtic Gods, Celtic Goddesses* (Cassell & Co., 2000, London)

Telesco, Patricia, *365 Goddess: A Daily Guide to the Magic and Inspiration of the Goddess* (HarperSanFrancisco, 1998, New York)

Trobe, Kala, *Invoke the Goddess: Visualizations of Hindu, Greek & Egyptian Deities* (Llewellyn Publications, 2000, St. Paul, MN)

Vessantara, *Meeting the Buddhas: A Guide to Buddhas, Bodhisattvas, and Tantric Deities* (Birmingham, England, 1998)

Yu, Chun-fang, *Kuan-yin: The Chinese Transformation of Avalokitesvara* (Columbia University Press, 2000, New York)

About the Author

Doreen Virtue, Ph.D., is a clairvoyant doctor of psychology and a fourth-generation metaphysician who works with the angelic, elemental, and ascended master realms in her writings and workshops. Doreen has lectured extensively throughout the world on topics related to her books, and she has appeared on many national and local television programs including *Oprah,* CNN, *Good Morning America, The View, Beyond with James Van Praagh,* and many more. She's the author of the bestselling *Healing with the Angels* and *Messages from Your Angels* books/angel cards. Website: **www.AngelTherapy.com**

We hope you enjoyed this Hay House book.
If you would like to receive a free catalog featuring additional
Hay House books and products, or if you would like
information about the Hay Foundation, please contact:

Hay House, Inc.
P.O. Box 5100
Carlsbad, CA 92018-5100

(760) 431-7695 or (800) 654-5126
(760) 431-6948 (fax) or (800) 650-5115 (fax)
www.hayhouse.com®

Published and distributed in Australia by:
Hay House Australia Pty. Ltd. • 18/36 Ralph St. • Alexandria NSW 2015
Phone: 612-9669-4299 • *Fax:* 612-9669-4144 • www.hayhouse.com.au

Published and distributed in the United Kingdom by:
Hay House UK, Ltd., 292B Kensal Rd., London W10 5BE•
Phone: 44-20-8962-1230 • *Fax:* 44-20-8962-1239
www.hayhouse.co.uk

Published and distributed in the Republic of South Africa by:
Hay House SA (Pty), Ltd., P.O. Box 990, Witkoppen 2068
Phone/Fax: 27-11-706-6612 • orders@psdprom.co.za

Published in India by:
Hay House Publications (India) Pvt. Ltd. • www.hayhouseindia.co.in

Distributed in India by:
Media Star, 7 Vaswani Mansion, 120 Dinshaw Vachha Rd.,
Churchgate, Mumbai 400020 • *Phone:* 91 (22) 22815538-39-40
Fax: 91 (22) 22839619 • booksdivision@mediastar.co.in

Distributed in Canada by:
Raincoast • 9050 Shaughnessy St., Vancouver, B.C. V6P 6E5
Phone: (604) 323-7100 • *Fax:* (604) 323-2600 • www.raincoast.com

Tune in to **HayHouseRadio.com®** for the best in inspirational talk radio featuring top
Hay House authors! And, sign up via the Hay House USA Website to receive the Hay House
online newsletter and stay informed about what's going on with your favorite authors.
You'll receive bimonthly announcements about: Discounts and Offers, Special Events,
Product Highlights, Free Excerpts, Giveaways, and more!
www.hayhouse.com®